Interpersonal Conflict

Interpersonal Conflict provides a psychotherapeutic and philosophical understanding of the nature of interpersonal conflict. Arguing that facilitating conflict resolution has little to do with objective logic or rationale, and everything to do with personal (and cultural) values and aspirations, Karen Weixel-Dixon uses the lens of existential psychotherapy to provide innovative skills for conflict management.

The book offers a deeper understanding of those theories and practices surrounding currently held perspectives on conflict, and extends the repertoire of communication skills relevant to difficult interpersonal situations, offering theoretical and practical input into the possibilities of reaching a therapeutic result.

Interpersonal Conflict will be an engaging and informative guide for professionals in psychotherapy, health, HR, legal, and teaching professions working with conflict, as well as students taking courses involving conflict resolution.

Karen Weixel-Dixon is a psychotherapist, supervisor, and accredited mediator in private practice, and a visiting lecturer at Regent's University London. She is co-director for Re-Solution Partnership.

Interpersonal Conflict

An Existential Psychotherapeutic and Practical Model

Karen Weixel-Dixon

LONDON AND NEW YORK

First published 2017
by Routledge
2 Park Square, Milton Park, Abingdon, Oxon OX14 4RN

and by Routledge
711 Third Avenue, New York, NY 10017

Routledge is an imprint of the Taylor & Francis Group, an informa business

© 2017 Karen Weixel-Dixon

The right of Karen Weixel-Dixon to be identified as author of this work
has been asserted by her in accordance with sections 77 and 78 of the
Copyright, Designs and Patents Act 1988.

All rights reserved. No part of this book may be reprinted or reproduced
or utilised in any form or by any electronic, mechanical, or other means,
now known or hereafter invented, including photocopying and recording,
or in any information storage or retrieval system, without permission in
writing from the publishers.

Trademark notice: Product or corporate names may be trademarks
or registered trademarks, and are used only for identification and
explanation without intent to infringe.

British Library Cataloguing in Publication Data
A catalogue record for this book is available from the British Library

Library of Congress Cataloging in Publication Data
Names: Weixel-Dixon, Karen, author.
Title: Interpersonal conflict: a psychotherapeutic and practical model /
    Karen Weixel-Dixon.
Description: Abingdon, Oxon; New York, NY: Routledge, 2017.
Identifiers: LCCN 2016022874 | ISBN 9781138195301 (hardback) |
    ISBN 9781138195318 (pbk.) | ISBN 9781315626437 (ebook)
Subjects: LCSH: Interpersonal conflict. | Existential psychotherapy.
Classification: LCC BF637.I48 W456 2015 | DDC 158.2—dc23
LC record available at https://lccn.loc.gov/2016022874

ISBN: 978-1-138-19530-1 (hbk)
ISBN: 978-1-138-19531-8 (pbk)
ISBN: 978-1-315-62643-7 (ebk)

Typeset in Times New Roman
by Swales & Willis Ltd, Exeter, Devon, UK

To my wonderful husband, Neil, who has always encouraged me to challenge my limitations and fulfil my possibilities.

Contents

About the author	ix
Acknowledgements	x
Introduction: The aim and structure of this book	1
1 Why existential psychotherapy?	5
2 The essence of conflict and resolution	11

PART I
Theoretical foundations — **15**

3 The givens of existence	19
4 The world-view	27
5 Self and other	33
6 Time and temporality	39
7 The contributions of phenomenology	45
8 The contributions of hermeneutics	51

Part I summary — **57**

Case vignette 1: The family — **61**

viii Contents

PART II
The practice of facilitative conflict resolution

73

  9 Attitudes about conflict and resolution   77

10 A theory of emotions and how to work with them   83

11 Practice and skills in managing conflict resolution   89

12 Strategies for facilitative conflict mediation   95

13 Format, protocol, and process for facilitative mediation   100

14 Ethical considerations for conflict and resolution   105

Part II summary   **111**

Case vignette 2: Unfair dismissal   **115**

    Conclusion   127
    Index   132

About the author

Karen Weixel-Dixon, M.A., Adv. Dip. Ex. Psych., Acc. Legal Mediator RUL, UKCP reg., EAP Cert. and reg., is an accredited psychotherapist, supervisor, trainer, and mediator in private practice, and has been a member of visiting faculty at Regent's University London since 1995. She also presents workshops and seminars for law firms, professional organisations, and educational institutions.

She maintains her work in both the UK and France, working with individuals, groups, families, and organisations.

The paradigm she favours is Existential Phenomenological, and she has a particular interest in how people experience, and engage with, temporality.

Karen has published papers in journals and textbooks in the field of psychotherapy, and most recently co-authored (with Susan Iacovou) *Existential Therapy: 100 Key Points and Techniques* (Routledge, 2015).

Karen has been a member of the Society for Existential Analysis since 1995, and was on the executive committee for ten years.

She presents CPD seminars on conflict, relationship therapy, and existential therapy as well as supervision and group work.

Acknowledgements

I would like to particularly acknowledge my friend and colleague Paul Randolph, who is always willing to discuss, challenge, and work through it; and I would also like to express my appreciation to the thousands of students who have privileged me with their feedback and engagement.

Introduction: The aim and structure of the book

The principle aim of this book is to offer readers the opportunity to consider their attitude towards, and understanding of, interpersonal conflict and resolution.

Existential works – philosophical, artistic, and fictional – provide the grounding for existential psychotherapy; both practices provide a basis for understanding the human predicament, which, of course, includes conflict.

Existentialism addresses the concerns that are common amongst all cultures and societies, and across all epochs; it is this universality that allows for a 'common ground' of understanding. It is a school of thought that is not particularly uniform, as there are variations in emphasis on different aspects of living. However, there are a few themes that are central to what is recognised as the existential perspective: freedom, choice, death, responsibility, embodiment, language, anxiety, uncertainty, time, meaninglessness, and change.

Human beings experience all these aspects: we live them. And, as human beings, our existence is 'in-the-world', always in context, and always in a world that is shared by others. It is within this sphere of inter-relatedness that conflict appears; this is why it is always personal. Even when we have a problem with an inanimate object, it is the *person* who is having the difficulty, not the object.

We are never completely alone, but neither are we ever completely fused with another human being. (Even if we withdraw from society, we still stand in relation to that from which we are apart.) As beings that are capable of, if not 'condemned' to, exercising freedom, sometimes in contradiction to an other's intentions, we stand as possible opponents to the will of another.

The 'givens of existence' as listed above are issues that are common to us all; how we *engage* with these aspects is what makes us all different.

2 Introduction

The result of this engagement is the 'world-view', comprising aspirations, expectations, and assumptions about ourselves, others, the world, and the cosmos.

Each of us is unique: no one else shares the particulars of their birth (where, how, and to which parents), or the exact time and place that they occupy right now; but we all share the same concerns.

And we may share similar hopes and ambitions, but *how these are realised*, or valued, can be the source of conflict.

Rollo May comments on these qualities:

> Does not every human conflict reveal universal characteristics of man as well as the idiosyncratic problems of the individual? (May 1969, p. 19)

We have a basis for understanding: we are all struggling with the same issues.

The first part of this book expands on the philosophical proposals from existential and phenomenological sources that are most relevant to the issue of conflict; the second half of the book offers a model for the exploration of the themes introduced, in terms of areas for self-reflection, and how to facilitate the same kind of enquiry with others.

The model for these explorations is based in on an attitude that is described as dialogical: a quality of being with others that promotes trust, and allows for the opportunity to discover and reveal aspects of the world-view that are implicated in the situation under consideration. The communication skills and strategies are not applied techniques, but rather extensions of the philosophical themes proposed. It is for this reason that they are grouped under the title of 'practice'.

Emotions, as the 'voices of values', are important indicators of personal investment in the situation: the desires and aspirations that are at risk in a conflict situation are disclosed in emotive expressions and communications; to ignore or distract from these is to lose essential information. How to explore these expressions, and how to appreciate the insight they provide, is considered an essential function of facilitation.

The format for a facilitated mediation process is outlined, but it is characterised as a most basic template that can be modified to suit the context and practicalities of the situation. It is considered to be most effective if the parties to a dispute have the opportunity to explore their concerns in confidential and private sessions with the facilitator; in these discussions, the covert and the overt 'agendas' of the party can be discovered, explored further, acknowledged, and understood in the context of current ambitions and hopes.

It may be apparent, even at this early stage, that what is being proposed in this exposition is that it is essential to hold some understanding about the human condition, and particularly inter-relatedness, if we hope to make the most of the *opportunity* that conflict can yield. People in dispute with one another are demonstrating that they care deeply about something. If these concerns are acknowledged, even if not agreed with, the possibilities for both cooperation and compromise may become more promising – and attractive – than remaining entrenched in an anxiety-provoking conflict.

The vignettes offered at the conclusion of each section are fictionalised accounts, meant to illustrate the typical themes and elements of disputes in general. They are compilations of scenarios that are meant to demonstrate the principles proposed, and do not refer to any specific event. The studies are each analysed for their relevance to some of the theoretical aspects introduced in this text, but a comprehensive representation of all the precepts discussed is beyond the scope of this project. However, I hope the reader finds them useful.

All conflicts are amenable to mediation, but not all parties to conflicts will be willing. In almost all mediations, one party or some people are more invested in a resolution, if not a reconciliation, than their opponents. Mediation may not provide the 'ideal' solution, but it can produce an agreement that allows for relationships to develop, instead of being destroyed. Inevitably, new conflicts will arise, but if one has experienced the positive effects of exploration, communication, and cooperation, then it is at least more likely that a negotiated agreement can be achieved.

In conclusion, I must acknowledge an obvious limitation of this work: the issue of violence.

When a person's (or a group's) aspirations and ambitions seem to be exclusively focused on a 'cosmological', or spiritual, level, it can be extremely difficult to promote the value of worldly aims and goals. It often appears that violence, when it is an attempt to 'actualise' these other-worldly purposes, is an action that relegates all mortal concerns.

However, even though it appears that the principles reviewed in this book do have some relevance in many situations of aggression, it is also apparent that violence is the preferred choice for some whose private logic is impenetrable, and who are impervious to entreaty.

4   Introduction

Such a significant and critical topic is beyond the scope of this text, and perhaps beyond the ability of this author: I leave this enquiry to the more intrepid explorers of the human condition.

Reference

May, R. 1969 *Love and Will*, Bantam Doubleday Dell, New York.

Chapter 1

Why existential psychotherapy?

Before we consider the question 'Why existential psychotherapy', it would be useful to give a brief overview of the philosophical school that underpins the psychotherapeutic model.

There are factors that are common to every human being: we are born, we die, we suffer, we change, we live (in) time, we strive, we inhabit a world with others. The list of what are known as 'existential givens' will be expanded as our discussion proceeds; suffice it to note at this point that we all share, in every epoch, culture, and place, the same conditions of existence.

It follows, then, that a basic appreciation of these aspects may deepen our understanding of ourselves and of others: we share the most fundamental concerns. It is precisely because we share these kinds of circumstances that there is a possibility of understanding each other at some level and to some extent. This is an important principle to be aware of when one is either a party to a dispute or acting as a facilitator to a disagreement: there is a principle involved, a value that is implicated in the positions that are being contested and defended; with some investigation and reflection, we can probably ascertain, and to some degree identify with, these issues.

To the extent that we can comprehend what is being thwarted in any contest, the situation can become less threatening to those involved or even to those observing: the ground may feel familiar, the issues recognised as those we have in common in some way.

It is often the case that it is *mis*-understanding that is at the core of interpersonal conflict; therefore, having even a modicum of comprehension about what one's opponent might be struggling with can provide a glimmer of hope for rapprochement (and possibly also manipulation, which will be considered subsequently).

6 Why existential psychotherapy?

Additionally, someone who is angry or defensive doesn't always have a clear or deep comprehension of the multiple issues and principles that are involved in their own complaint; they are too busy trying to camouflage what they believe to be their vulnerabilities.

The concerns expressed in any contest can be recognised as deeply human. This helps to *normalise* the situation, and can open the way for it to be viewed as an opportunity for communication and development in a relationship.

Furthermore, it stands to reason that as these concerns are recognisable as universal, it does not require any particular expertise or specialist training to appreciate the interests that are common between all people(s).

Existential philosophy, as a body of works, considers the human condition in an attempt to reach a description of the needs and concerns that *make us* human. An aspect of being human is also being unique: we each hold a particular perspective on our common predicament.

Rollo May comments on the relevance of existential psychology:

> *Existentialism deepens the concepts that define the human condition*. In so doing, it prepares the way (for the first time) *for a psychology of mankind*. (May 1969, p. 94)

This is a fundamentally inclusive perspective.

Though existential philosophy is often described as a school of thought that is as disparate as it is cohesive, the principle unifying factor under consideration by the existentialists is described by Friedman:

> the actual situation of the existential subject as the starting point of thought. (Friedman 1992, p. 4)

The focus is on this person before us, and with us: this person is the example of how we are all the same, *and* different.

Existential philosophy is not just armchair rhetoric: the greatest minds of this school of thought used their own lives and experiences as the starting point for the exploration of what it means to be human, of what it means to exist. Nietzsche, Kierkegaard, Sartre, Heidegger, and Merleau-Ponty are but a few of the writers and thinkers that are included in this group, and all of them looked to the concrete and the particular in their lives in the hopes of understanding human existence. (It should be noted that existentialist works are not just philosophical; Franz Kafka would be an example of this, as would be the dramas of Sartre.)

In an overview of the considerations explored by these philosophical expositions, it is noted that all human cultures entertain similar questions: How shall I live? Why do I exist, and die? What difference does my life make, if any? The enquiries are ubiquitous; the response is personal. There are no abstract responses to these questions: the answers are demonstrated in our choices, our behaviours, what we would live for, die for, and fight for.

In this way, existential philosophy is recognised as an investigation that begins with a *subject*, that is, the human subject.

Macquarrie also comments on this aspect of the philosophy:

> It is a philosophy of the subject rather than the object. (Macquarrie 1973, p. 14)

So although we do all share some basic concerns, we also hold a *unique* perspective on these concerns. This is what is meant by subjective truth (this theme will be expanded upon in later chapters of this text).

What makes this a particularly important perspective for understanding interpersonal conflict is that these kinds of challenges are the result of *seemingly* opposing views of 'truth', subjective truths, each held passionately, each defended vigorously. These views may not be fully articulated or appreciated by those involved, even though they may be the basis of the individual's (or the group's) choice or their own position; but the crisis can be the opportunity for just such revelations.

As I often comment to those studying conflict and mediation, the dispute is not *in the paperwork*; it is *between* the people involved. The 'truth' of the matter is not represented by objective facts, but how the facts are subjectively experienced. To discover that truth, one has to explore; one has to enquire.

It should be noted, however, that subjective truth is not a license to justify any choice or action. We share a world with others; they will be affected by each individual's action (in word and deed); and subsequently will bear further consequences for (possibly) everyone within a particular context or network.

This stance is in opposition to abstract analyses and scientific paradigms that seek to define humans in a reistic, mechanistic model. In other words, we must look to the being himself to understand how his life is being experienced, and how his values inform his choices. It is difficult, and ineffective, to attempt to understand a person from an objective standpoint, for example, via the structure of the brain. Although there may be some scientific validity in such a description (and this may

8 Why existential psychotherapy?

be helpful in some contexts), it does not account for the person's perspective on their situation, which is what lies at the heart of their value system, and therefore their strategies for actualising these values.

Existential psychotherapy, which forms the basis for this paradigm of understanding and managing interpersonal conflict, is itself grounded in the tenets of existential philosophy. The psychotherapy is *not* so much an applied philosophical model as it is a project in understanding any person, and any people, with reference to the concerns that are common to all human beings, and how these issues are being *met* and engaged with by this particular individual or group.

As there is an expectation of some shift in perspective for those involved in a dispute, there is also hope in existential therapy for change. This change will likely be in the form of awareness, and understanding of self in relation to others and to the conditions of existence. The aim is for clarity about one's engagements with these givens, and an appreciation of one's agency.

Deurzen-Smith comments:

> The existential approach to counselling centres on an exploration of someone's particular way of seeing life, the world and herself . . . in reconsidering what was previously thought of as already known certain fresh discoveries are made. (Deurzen-Smith 1988, p. 26)

These discoveries cannot but help to shift perspectives: new awareness produces further options, and some possible choices are also eliminated by virtue of practical circumstances, or voluntarily discarded. Already, we can see the possibility for change of some description.

The agency, the exercise of choice, will be in the service of how we respond to these givens; our choices will support our assumptions about how we can best engage with the conditions for the betterment of our lives, and the realisation of our values. This is an issue that will be elucidated throughout these discussions.

Cohn comments further on the aims of therapy:

> Existential therapy may see as its aim to help the clients to free themselves from the disturbing consequences of denial, evasion and distraction by enabling them to change their response to the existential givens. (Cohn 1997, p. 24)

A change in response to the givens may not lead to a change in behaviour: one may recognise the purpose(s) for one's choice in behaviour,

Why existential psychotherapy?   9

and continue in the same behavioural strategies; what is of paramount significance is that one recognises *the choosing*.

A few of the givens that are most often implicated in conflict situations are responsibility, freedom, and choice. These are conditions that are both blessings and burdens: we often look to someone else to make decisions for us, to assume responsibility (or liability) for our predicament, and we often insist that we are shackle-bound to our course of action.

Certainly, parties in a dispute will often hope to assign the responsibility for the outcome of the difficult situation onto a well-meaning spectator, or facilitator, or to circumstances that are described as 'beyond one's control'.

However, if, either as a party to a dispute or as a facilitator for resolution, one can always bear in mind the personal, subjective nature of the situation, one cannot fail to recognise that as the contest *is always personal*, so must the settlement be: the agreement must be a creation that addresses the needs and desires that are particularly relevant to these persons, at this time, and in this context.

This gives us an indication as to the nature of what may be described as a *facilitative* resolution process, even when the facilitator is one or both of the parties involved; it is the revelation, discovery, and acknowledgement of the most personal elements of any conflict that promotes the possibility of a therapeutic outcome to the exchange.

The process of facilitative resolution is one in which the values and principles of the people involved in the conflict, that is, their worldviews, are recognised for their relevance to the situation at hand, which is the current dispute. It is ineffective in an interpersonal conflict, much as it is in therapy, for anyone not directly invested in the outcome of the process to offer, or attempt to impose, their own or any source of external evaluation or rationale for understanding the disagreement, or for the creation of the resolution: such a strategy would in fact *de-personalise* the process, and possibly derail it as well.

Keeping it personal means keeping it relevant to these specific individuals embroiled in this dilemma; it is this quality that allows for a therapeutic effect, in that the needs of these parties will have to be served to some extent. *How* this occurs, in terms of particulars and practicalities, will also be a direct expression of their own intentions and ambitions.

For the most part, what is being facilitated is *clarification* and *communication*: clarification of what is at stake, and the timely and sensitive communication, to the others involved, of these concerns.

Parties to a conflict, in the course of this process, begin to realise that there is some possibility of satisfaction of at least some of their needs

10 Why existential psychotherapy?

and wishes, which is quite a different horizon than that of the intransigent positions that are commonly the starting point of a dispute.

The clarification of one's world-view allows one to recognise the values that are reflected in our choices, as well as what strategies we employ in an effort to actualise these values and intentions. When these strategies are met with resistance, from another person for example, or are impeded by any element, we become frustrated at least, and can become more aggressive, or manipulative, in an effort to actualise these values and intentions.

References

Cohn, H.W. 1997 *Existential Thought and Therapeutic Practice: An introduction to existential psychotherapy,* Sage, London.

Deurzen-Smith, E. van 1988 *Existential Counselling in Practice*, Sage, London.

Friedman, M. 1992 *The Worlds of Existentialism: A critical reader,* Humanities Press International, Atlantic Highlands, NJ.

Macquarrie, J. (1972) 1973 *Existentialism*, Penguin Books, London.

May R. (1961) 1969 *Existential Psychology* (ed. R. May), McGraw-Hill, New York.

Chapter 2

The essence of conflict and resolution

It's always personal. Conflict involves at least one person, and more commonly more than one, but even when it is an individual in a contest with their computer, it is the particular world-view of that individual that is being challenged.

It is paramount to keep this proposal at the forefront of this discussion. When one is confronted with what seems to be the faceless facade of a corporation, or the aloof demeanour of a representative of an organisation, one must recall that the aims of these entities are, in the final analysis, represented by and grounded in very human issues. On those occasions when one feels powerless to persuade or assuage the other, be they individuals or conglomerates, the advantage lies in making it personal and keeping it personal. The how and why of this approach will be a central theme in this text.

There would be no conflict if disputes could be settled 'rationally', or logistically. It is often the case that those who are not party to the actual disagreement feel that they have a reasonable and objective means by which to fairly resolve the situation, and they stand by in wonder at the seeming irrationality of the combatants. It has been suggested that if the details of the stand-off could be fed to a computer or some other form of artificial intelligence, the mechanism could probably arrive at a settlement that would appear to be legal, equitable, and comprehensible.

It has also been proposed that conflicts could be remedied by an objective, unbiased third party who has no investment in the outcome of the situation. The notions of objectivity and impartiality will be examined in this book, and the reader may come to appreciate that such qualities are aspirational, but not entirely achievable, and perhaps not as desirable as they might seem to be.

Fundamentally, in the most violent contest or in the more discrete disagreement, one side wants something the other side will not give. This is the

12   Essence of conflict and resolution

nature of conflict, in all circumstances, across all eras. All parties believe to some large extent that their position is justified; if the other side cannot comprehend the righteousness of their position, then they are 'deluded', 'ill-informed', or purely obstinate or evil (these qualifications will be extended to observers who do not share the proposed rationale, even if these include high court judges). By virtue of such a perspective, the contenders often believe that the opponent is the author of their own misery, and possibly their destruction: that is, they are bringing it upon themselves.

It is often the case that those involved in a disagreement had no original intention to enter into a combative situation: they may feel that they have been drawn into the situation in an effort to defend another, or have been implicated purely by accident. There is generally, in any case, a sense that the situation is unfair: the people on the other side want something they do not deserve; the people grouped together are being treated unfairly, and their intentions are misconstrued by the others; or fate has also contributed in some way that provoked an unjust predicament.

In the case of a misfortune, we are confronted with our lack of control over many circumstances. We can feel de-personalised and dis-empowered in these occurrences. For example, when a violent storm uproots a great oak that falls onto a neighbour's house, causing extensive damage to the building, it may seem unfair to expect the owner of the tree that pre-dates his habitation by decades to assume responsibility for the occurrence. The home-owner whose property is damaged, however, sees no other source of blame and restitution for the problem, and feels perfectly justified in claiming expenses for repairs from his neighbour. The legalities of the situation aside, the premise of the dispute becomes a very human issue: when we suffer and feel it is not our own fault, we want compensation of some sort; otherwise, the situation remains unfair, and we are reminded of our impotence in the face of natural forces.

When people enter into, or find themselves embroiled in, a dispute, they may react with incredulity, defensiveness, submission, aggression, or retreat. The immediate reaction will be relevant to the context, and particularly to the people involved in this specific event.

As an illustration, if I am standing in line for the grocery store checkout and someone remarks that I am not suitably dressed to appear in public, I am likely to be only moderately disturbed by their disapprobation, but if my partner questions my dress sense on the way to a family gathering, I am more likely to react with dismay and anger. In the first context, there is little risk of loss of dignity or self-esteem; in the second scenario, I have potentially a great deal to lose, and my emotional reaction will be quite different. What this emotional reaction demonstrates in terms of my world-view and how aspects of it are implicated in this interaction will be explored in the following chapters.

The difference between the two scenarios related above may be obvious: I have a greater emotional and value-laden investment in the view expressed by my partner. I *care* a great deal more about my partner's perspective than that of a stranger or a mere acquaintance because there is a greater *loss* implicated in his negative evaluation: he sees me in a way that is not acceptable to him and there is a possibility that he may reject me, or, in the worst-case scenario, his affection for me might diminish and I will be abandoned.

Similar principles are in operation between warring groups of people.

When one group enters into conflict with another, it is an attempt to acquire, protect, stabilise, or eliminate some position, object(s) (including people), or condition. People group together to consolidate what power and resources they have at their disposal to conquer or persuade the opposing group to concede to their intentions. The force that is levied in these combative situations is commensurate with the threat of loss and the value placed on the object of that possible loss.

So the initial principle of conflict is denial of the fulfilment of the needs and/or desires of another person, or persons, by an individual or a group.

To observers, and indeed often to those embroiled in the conflict, the dispute may seem irrational; the arguments may appear to be resistant to 'objective' input, and there is a sense for those locked in battle that they are the 'reasonable' coalition and that injustice is the product of the opposition's recalcitrance.

How such disputes are and have been settled has depended upon the wisdom and charity, or lack thereof, of the affected individuals. Obviously, wars, disputes, contests, and conflicts of all types are 'resolved' by sheer might (legal, financial, or military, for example) in many circumstances, or via negotiation in some scenarios. But while negotiation may be preferable to violence or coercion, it often leaves those involved with an unsatisfactory result: the moral high ground is left unattended to, and the values that were meant to be revered and served have been compromised, if not ravaged.

It is the blockage to the realisation of the personal values that are reflected in the party's world-view that is the issue at the heart of every conflict. It is this seat of 'private logic' that is seemingly impervious to the influence or persuasion of would-be arbitrators or well-meaning negotiators.

The type of conflict resolution that is being promoted in this book is one that can only be the result of true dialogue and engagement.

14 Essence of conflict and resolution

In keeping with the proposal that *it is always personal*, agreement that is created in a facilitated mediation founded in the psychotherapeutic and philosophical tenets espoused in the following pages will also be equally personal: it will more sufficiently reflect the world-views – the personal perspectives – of those involved. These elements are what clarify the possible gratification in creating a resolution.

Consequently, the resolution will be *owned* by the parties involved: it will serve, to some greater extent, the values and principles that are important to the people constructing the agreement.

The qualities of engagement and the skills that support true dialogue will be elaborated throughout this text. It is important to note here that this process is more of an art than a science. There are no hard and fast rules of procedure as there are in the legal system or in a scientific endeavour. What is being proposed is that a quality of listening to – of being-with – those involved in a dispute will clarify what is most important for them: what may be gained, what may be lost, and what they are willing to give and lose to achieve the realisation of the values they hold most dear. The people who appear locked in a stagnant situation of fear and defensiveness will be allowed to discover the sources of their anxieties, and to acquire the power to attend to them.

This is not a promise of 'win-win' (there will be some discussion as to why that is not possible outcome), but it is an assertion that a more satisfactory settlement for all is more likely to be reached via cooperation than through coercion.

Conflict is an inevitable aspect of the human condition. It is the subject of religious tenets; political agendas; cultural, sociological, and psychological studies; and evolutionary theories. It has been explored in the earliest writings of the pre-Socratics and in the ancient texts of Far Eastern philosophy.

Conflict can be a powerful source of communication; it may also be a source of greater self-awareness. It is the point in a dialogue in which the volume is raised, the interest is focused, and the need to communicate is dramatic and dramatised.

If one can become sensitive to one's own need to communicate a message that is not being received, and to the strategies one develops to make that happen, the episode can produce a level of self-awareness that might otherwise remain latent. In those moments when we intensely wish our position to be understood, even if not agreed with, we can discover what is most important us, and what we may be willing to sacrifice in order to actualise that value. How to develop this self-awareness, and how to deepen our comprehension of the other's intentions, will be discussed at length in this text.

Part I

Theoretical foundations

The foundations of the existential model of psychotherapy are no more cohesive than the philosophical sources: there are few 'absolutes' in this perspective, for reasons we will discover later, and this attitude is evident in existentialism in general.

It should be noted that no modern philosophy stands alone. Philosophers are influenced by and benefit from thinkers that precede them, from traditions that pre-date their own era, and from cultures that existed well before their own time. Friedman notes:

> The list of those who might be considered forerunners of modern existentialism is inexhaustible. (Friedman 1992, p. 5)

Indeed, Friedman's formidable text (1992) references Greek philosophy, the Bible, and early Hassidic sources in his review of early foundations for existential thought.

As it is with the philosophical background, so it is with the psychotherapeutic model: the variety of perspectives is notable. Cooper (2003) refers to a 'rich tapestry of existential therapies', Friedman (1992) refers to the philosophy as a 'mood', and Spinelli (2007) alludes to 'an existential attitude'. It is understandable, therefore, that any exposition on the topics will provide only a sketch, a background, for further study and reflection.

The following subheadings offer an overview of topics, themes, and concerns that are favoured in the existential paradigm; in various schools of thought there may be emphasis on particular aspects. This text seeks to emphasise those elements that are particularly relevant to the understanding and psychotherapeutic management of conflict and facilitated resolution.

In almost all the philosophical as well as the fictional writings characterised as existential, there are aspects of human existence that are

16   Part I: Theoretical foundations

commonly referenced: freedom, responsibility, choice, death, time, and – what is considered a more inclusive designation – being-in-the-world. These elements are characterised as givens, or the 'ontological' aspects; how each of us responds to these aspects is characterised as 'ontic'.

These 'givens' of human existence can be readily appreciated as concerns that are reflected in every culture, in every epoch, and it is this quality of shared interests that qualifies existential psychotherapy as an effective approach for understanding life, humanity, and relationships. It follows, then, that it is likely we will find some understanding of the cycle of conflict and resolution that appears throughout all cultural and personal histories.

However, the philosophy does not instruct the practitioner; it *informs* the practitioner. The *how* of existential practice is an extension of the understanding of the human predicament. There will be much discussion in this book as to the attitude, or an approach rather than a technique, that best serves an inquiry of how perceptions are being valued and how situations, especially relationships, are being experienced.

With this in mind, both philosophers and practitioners will be referenced for their wisdom on the subject of conflict and resolution.

Søren Kierkegaard (1813–1855) is widely recognised as one of the key contributors to existential thought. Kierkegaard rejected the glorification of scientific paradigms and looked to the individual to abide in his own 'truth'. It is not enough to have codes of conduct, religious or political, that can be relied on to provide answers to how one lives one's life; to be ethical, to *stand in* the truth, one must choose for oneself how to act on and in the world. This is known as an ethical paradigm, and the proposals resonate deeply with themes of choice, freedom, and responsibility.

This concern is readily apparent in conflict situations with respect to one's commitment to one's own truth, and one's subjective view of justice and righteousness; however, this does not grant carte blanche to impose one's perspective on others, as others also have a privileged position on their own interpretation of truth.

Friedrich Nietzsche (1844–1900) is known for his emphasis on the singular responsibility of man in terms of his ethical and moral position. Rollo May proposes:

> Nietzsche was more accurate when he described Man as the organism who makes certain values – prestige, power, tenderness, love – more important than pleasure and even more important than survival itself. (May 1969, p. 18)

Part I: Theoretical foundations 17

Here we have the voice of the prophet Nietzsche who proclaims that we cannot turn to a universal source for justification of our choices: each must create their own set of values, principles that are arbitrary and contingent, without the validation of a higher authority. As we shall see, these values, and the aspirations to have them actualised, are the source of collaboration and of conflict.

Nietzsche also asserts that we do not have access to any ultimate truth or morality as opposed to those views held by others, and we must recognise that we are highly motivated to actualise the values we have chosen with very practical and political means.

Martin Heidegger (1889–1976) made distinguished contributions to phenomenology and hermeneutics, and attempted to present a comprehensive description of what it means to be a human existent. His proposal that we inhabit a 'with-world' indicates that we 'dwell' in a context that is relational and inter-subjective; we can have no detached or objective view on ourselves, our situation, or others. Cohn elaborates further:

> By being part of this context we also co-create it. (Cohn 2002, p. 104)

This means that we respond to all (and everyone) that meets us, thereby co-constituting our existence. This principle is particularly relevant to those occasions when we find ourselves embroiled in any uncomfortable situation, including disputes. How we have contributed to our own problems is always a useful inquiry; it can grant a sense of agency in what might at first look like a no-win situation.

Heidegger placed time at the centre of human affairs, with its implications for finitude, choice, responsibility, anxiety, guilt, language, and death. How we 'spend' our time, the irreplaceable resource, can be a significant consideration in all our choices, not least of all in how we choose to engage in the cycle of conflict and reconciliation.

Jean Paul Sartre (1905–1980) is well known for his treatise on freedom and responsibility, and the 'nothingness' that is at the core of selfhood and human existence, in his seminal work *Being and Nothingness* (1993).

But it is often his dramas that give a richer illustration of how we are affected by being-with-others. In *Huis Clos*, Sartre (2000) famously describes the reality of the inherent relatedness of our existence with the notion that 'Hell is other people'.

What makes this particularly relevant to conflict is that it is other people who can offer cooperation or resistance to our intentions: the ambitions to

18   Part I: Theoretical foundations

have our world-view realised, acknowledged, and validated. To the extent that anyone assists another in actualising their assumptions and expectations of themselves, of others, of the world in general, and of the cosmos at large, there will be peace and harmony, even love; to the extent that these aspirations are impeded, there will be conflict, and even war. He takes this principle to something of an extreme:

> Conflict is the original meaning of being-for-others. (Sartre 1993, p. 364)

Sartre's outlook is not without hope, but his perspectives are challenging, and enlightening.

This is a very brief overview of four of the key thinkers who are recognised as founders of existential philosophy in its modern context. Many authors, including poets and dramatists, philosophers, and practitioners from various sociological and psychological paradigms, have made notable contributions to an appreciation of the human condition. The inquiry continues, and conclusions should not mark the termination of our thinking.

References

Cohn, H.W. 2002 *Heidegger and the Roots of Psychotherapy*, Continuum, London.

Cooper, M. 2003 *Existential Therapies*, Sage, London.

Friedman, M. 1992 *The Worlds of Existentialism: A critical reader*, Humanities Press International, Atlantic Highlands, NJ.

May, R. (ed.) (1961) 1969 *Existential Psychology*, McGraw-Hill, New York.

Sartre, J.P. (1943) 1993 *Being and Nothingness* (trans. H.E. Barnes), Routledge, London.

Sartre, J.P. 2000 Huis Clos *and Other Plays*, Penguin Classics, London.

Spinelli, E. 2007 *Practising Existential Psychotherapy: The relational world*, Sage, London.

Chapter 3

The givens of existence

The givens of existence are those conditions of human existence that are common to all epochs and cultures. The givens that are reviewed here are highlighted as those that are particularly relevant for understanding and working with interpersonal conflict; this is not a comprehensive or definitive collection.

These aspects are demonstrated on the graph included, the existential circle of interrelated givens. The wheel is indicative of the non-sequential and co-related nature of these elements.

Time is at the centre of the wheel as the imposing factor for all the givens: it impacts on every other aspect. Time is often referred to as 'temporality', indicating that it is *how we experience* time in our lives, as well as how it is referenced collectively, that is the meaningful source of reflection. This aspect will be explored further in a subsequent section.

It is difficult to discuss any one given without implicating another. For example, if one considers embodiment to be an issue for any given human being, it is likely that death will be a related concern, as this event represents the termination of the body; but death will also have repercussions for relationship, as it also looms as the absolute separation; and of course, temporality underpins these concerns.

Each of these issues gives rise to themes that are readily recognised in a conflict situation. Exploring them will give the reader a solid grounding in the nature of conflict, and possibilities for therapeutic resolution.

'Relatedness' seems an obvious place to start, as it is a necessary ingredient for interpersonal conflict.

The term 'relatedness' is employed over that of 'relationship' to differentiate it from the notion of romantic entanglement; the former word indicates the full range of human engagements possible. These engagements include conflict and cooperation as well as all of the love/hate,

20 Givens of existence

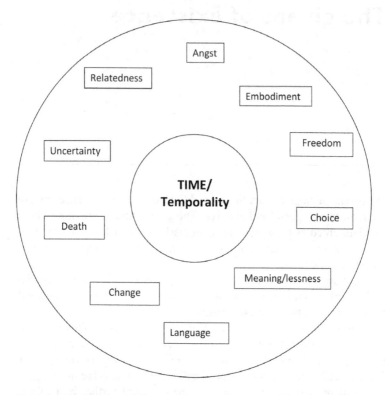

Figure 3.1 The Existential Givens of Human Existence: all are inter-related
©Karen Weixel-Dixon, 2011

acceptance/rejecting, and various other permutations of relationship that are possible between any dyad and amongst any group of people.

As a given of existence, it is *not* possible to be totally isolated, nor is it possible to be *fused* with another person; we stand always in relatedness, in some form.

Bugental comments on this 'a-partness', and he clarifies the dimensions as 'a-part-of and apart-from' (Bugental 1992, p. 239), which are the poles of possibility on the continuum of relatedness, between complete fusion and absolute isolation, neither of which is possible.

As a theme, this issue is often represented by the *necessity* as well as the inevitability of relatedness: we need others to help us actualise our intentions, but others can also act as impediments to these ambitions. In any case, others are *there*, helping, hindering, and judging.

Freedom is a central issue in all existential works, fictional as well as philosophical. It also has significant repercussions for therapy, and certainly for conflict.

Freedom, like choice, which is a closely related issue, is both a burden and a blessing: it is wonderful to have options, but in realising any option, we exclude others. Additionally, freedom imbues us with possibilities, but also liabilities: we stand alone in our responsibility for choosing one thing and not another. It is of little use (in persuading others) or consolation to ascribe our choice to the influence of others, or society, or circumstances, or human nature, or character traits (although, of course, these are the kinds of explanations offered when our choices result in undesirable outcomes).

Additionally, we have much evidence in our lives that even with the best intentions, our choices do not always produce the desired or anticipated results. We cannot know ahead of time what the 'right' choice is. There is also ample evidence to demonstrate that what was once considered a 'good' or a 'bad' decision may be re-evaluated, upon subsequent review, to be the exact opposite. Again, we are left bewildered as to how best to choose the next time.

It should be noted that freedom does *not* mean that all options are available. Freedom is always contextualised within parameters and with reference to limitations, that is, those imagined options that *cannot* be chosen. An example of this would be a desire to change past events – those 'facts' are immutable.

It is enough at this point to note that although freedom and the correlate of choice is a principle cherished in all societies (in some form), it is understandably fraught with anxiety.

We can appreciate that we feel anxious as an emotional response to freedom and choice, and the attendant uncertainty, but there is also a kind of anxiety that is considered a given of existence, and as such, it is referred to as 'angst', or existential anxiety.

Angst hovers in the background of all our activities. It is sometimes dim, occasionally intrusive, but it seems impossible to pinpoint the exact source; it is everywhere, and nowhere.

Heidegger proposes:

> That in the face of which one is anxious is completely indefinite. (Heidegger 1993, p. 231)

We exist in a continuous state of existential anxiety. No explanation of what the source of this anxiety might be is ever fully satisfactory, but it has a profound effect on us.

22 Givens of existence

Polt (1999) gives an example of someone going about their daily chores – the shopping, and the gardening, activities that have meaning and provide order in one's life – when the realisation arrives that there is no point to all this, in the grand scheme of things. We might query: will it make a great difference if I do this, or that, today or tomorrow?

He continues:

> The security of everyday existence, in which the meaning of life seems well-grounded and obvious, has been shattered. (Polt 1999, p. 77)

It is Being itself that un-nerves us; it is contingent, that is, *it could all be otherwise*. I might not have been born, and I might die at any moment; I might have been born somewhere other than where I was born, or at some other time; I might not be able to bring about the future that I cherish for myself and my loved ones.

In acknowledging such contingencies, we are confronted with meaninglessness. Even if one subscribes to a divine order, it is a belief that could be revoked, or reinvested, modified, or abandoned. If one chooses to believe, in anything, one does so in an act of faith, and faith without doubt is hollow.

In these moments, we stand alone in the face of having to choose, of being responsible, and of creating (or choosing) our own meanings.

However, we cannot remain in this limbo for long; we need meaning to give us some grounding in the face of such contingency, even if it seems to be a delusion. It would be impossible to stay with the chaos that meaninglessness implies; we impose order on our lives just to be able to move from one place to another. In so doing, we create values in our choice of meanings; we make something valuable by virtue of having chosen it. Furthermore, as we shall discover, it is because one can choose that both conflict and resolution are inevitable.

Anxiety, therefore, although an uncomfortable experience, re-awakens us to the flexible, groundless contingency of our existence. For as long as we can remain with, or even acknowledge, this situation, we can authentically exercise our freedom, our agency, and our responsibility.

The discomfort that is a consequence of the realisation of contingency is also a product of uncertainty. We have already encountered this quality with respect to the uncertainty attached to choices.

Uncertainty pervades human existence. We do not know when or how we will die, only that we will; we cannot control the forces of Nature, which can upset any human-made plans and ambitions; and certainly

Givens of existence   23

we are too often in error in deciphering the inclinations and intentions of others.

As with meaning/lessness, we need some basis for managing our way in the world, so we make assumptions to contend with uncertainty. Although it is understandable that we come to rely on our assumptions, it can be problematic when we begin to act as though these are universal truths.

The implications of this proclivity for speculations and conjecture, which is a wondrous faculty in human beings, will be explored in greater depth under the topics of hermeneutics and phenomenology. For the sake of our interest in interpersonal conflict, it can be anticipated that it is often mistaken or malformed assumptions that both cause and maintain disputes.

Assumptions, of course, are present in thought; thought, in turn, is expressed in language. Language is the manner in which we articulate and communicate our thoughts.

Language is not just about words; it is about being-in-the-world with others, and as such it is considered a given of existence by most existential thinkers.

It is through language that thought becomes public and accessible, and this is essential to our being-in-the-world. (Macquarrie 1973, p. 144).

Being-in-the-world-with-others is a shared existence – again, shared, but not in exactly the same way for everyone; it is just these commonalities and distinctions that we attempt to communicate with language.

Gadamer suggests:

> He [any person] can make what is not present manifest . . . so that another person sees it before him. (Gadamer 2008, p. 60)

So language allows us to share our perspectives, and certainly this is relevant to interpersonal conflict, as the need to communicate their perspectives, and to enforce them, is the aim of the contestants.

However, language, from a philosophical perspective, does not result in absolute precision; it reveals and conceals simultaneously. The result can be understanding, but an understanding that is limited and temporary, even if it is momentarily satisfying.

Harding comments on this quality:

> here we can use the image of a light which draws out attention to one aspect of the world, but leaves the rest in darkness. (Harding 2005, p. 95)

24   Givens of existence

Language concerns more than words; it is about a shared understanding that develops, unfolds, and continues indefinitely. The implications of this will be expanded upon as we proceed.

Embodiment – being a body and having a body (Macquarrie 1973) – is the means by which I can be in the world: I can act on it, I can respond to my environment, and I am aware by virtue of embodiment. I am also in-the-world with others: I have a unique perspective on others, and they have a particular point-of-view on me that is, in part, a consequence of our spatial and temporal position.

The existential school of thought does not accord with Cartesian duality. Body and mind, or body and psyche, are aspects of a whole; they are different, but not separate.

Cohn states:

> body and mind are both parts of a total situation, they are both aspects of the phenomenon we perceive, and to look at them separately is to miss the full meaning of what we meet. (Cohn 2002, p. 54)

This view will be developed further under the next topic heading. However, one of the principle effects of embodiment is that it too represents limitations to our information and to our comprehension.

Embodiment also serves as a dramatic reminder for another existential given: change. It would be difficult to imagine anyone who does not notice, with some trepidation, the effects of ageing, of illness, of accidents, on the body; then again, the changes in the seasons are markers of how time changes everything: us, others, and our environment.

But more often than not, what we fear more than those changes that are beyond our control are those that are unpredictable. This aspect of existence connects also to that of uncertainty, as well as to freedom and choice, death, and time.

We can look into our own lives and note changes that we welcomed, some of which endured as blessings, and recall as well those vagaries that took us by surprise, and left us with the challenge of how to meet these transformations.

What most of us experience as particularly challenging is to have the desire or need to change, in terms of behaviour, for example, and yet not to have the 'willpower' to effect this intention. Additionally, we may also become exasperated, if not frustrated and angry, at others for failing to actualise a change that they, or others, or we, deem necessary or desirable.

These latter concerns can be appreciated readily for their relevance to interpersonal conflict. In the first instance, the opposing parties intend for the other side to change; what is being avoided is consideration of the idea that change may also have to originate with oneself, thereby effecting a *loss*, or at least a compromise, of one's own values and intentions.

This is at the heart of our trepidation in regard to change. There is always a loss incurred in change; the status quo ceases to exist, and a new situation arrives. This is a perpetual cycle.

This leads us to the final aspect of the wheel of existential givens: death. This is the ultimate change. Even if one subscribes to a belief in an afterlife, it will not be a fully 'human' existence.

Death is more than a clinical event; it is an eventuality, and a possibility. It is an end to all our possibilities, and an end to being human as we experience it; it is also a possibility at any given instant as we do not know when or how we will expire.

As mortals, we cannot fully grasp the concept of our own death, but we witness the inevitable via the demise of others. However, we can apprehend that when our time comes, this is an occurrence that is ours alone; we may have bedside companions, but the end is unequivocally one's own.

In recognising one's 'ownmost possibility' (Heidegger 1993), one may shed the interests and preoccupations that serve as diversions from this realisation, and become aware with a dramatic affect that one is ultimately responsible for one's own quality of existence. This could be described as an episode of authenticity.

This can be a distinctly liberating and/or intimidating event, as Boss describes it:

> If man were not finite and mortal . . . there would always be time to catch up and make something good. But for someone who is mortal, no situation happens twice in quite the same way. If what he does is not in tune with the moment, that moment is irrevocably lost to him . . . (Boss 1994, p. 121)

Such an engagement with death and mortality can serve to clarify for us just what is important, and what might be relegated, and what is worth the investment of one's finite resources – all very appropriate considerations for conflict dilemmas, as well as for life.

References

Boss, M. (1979) 1994 *Existential Foundations of Medicine and Psychology*, Aronson, Northvale, NJ.

Bugental, J.F.T. (1987) 1992 *The Art of the Psychotherapist: How to develop skills that take psychotherapy beyond science*, Norton, New York.

26 Givens of existence

Cohn, H.W. 2002 *Heidegger and the Roots of Existential Therapy*, Continuum, London.

Gadamer, H.-G. (1977) 2008 *Philosophical Hermeneutics* (trans. D.E. Linge), University of California Press, Los Angeles.

Harding, M. 2005 'Language', in *Existential Perspectives on Human Issues* (E. van Deurzen and C. Arnold-Baker, eds.), Palgrave Macmillan, Hampshire, UK.

Heidegger, M. (1962) 1993 *Being and Time* (trans. J. Macquarrie and E. Robinson), Blackwell, Oxford.

Macquarrie, J. (1972) 1973 *Existentialism*, Penguin Books, London.

Polt, R. 1999 *Heidegger: An introduction*, UCL Press, London.

Chapter 4

The world-view

Much has been made so far of the givens of existence as they pertain to all of us. This hopefully serves to facilitate a deeper understanding of how we all exist, and how much common ground we share. It is hoped that the discussions so far have demonstrated that we exist for and with each other; life is communal, globally as well as locally.

The world-view, in contrast, is the manifestation of how we are all unique. Here resides the 'private logic' that reflects the manner in which each of us engages with the givens of existence. As was proposed earlier, it is in our response to the 'invariables' of life that we exercise our freedom.

The world-view is a concept that was offered by the psychiatrist Ludwig Binswanger (May 1961) in a structured format: the Umwelt, the biological and environmental aspect; the Mitwelt, the 'with-world' of others like oneself; the Eigenwelt, the 'own-world' of relationship to oneself.

These dimensions were elucidated and expanded by Deurzen-Smith to include the Uberwelt, which refers to 'a person's connection to the abstract and the absolute aspect of living' (Deurzen-Smith 1988, p. 97).

Some of these categories are also reflected in the figures presented by Strasser and Randolph (2004), although those illustrations indicate a limited number of givens and strategies for engaging with the givens that are commonly observed in conflict.

The structure of the world-view as presented here is simplified, and indicates that these categories are inter-connected and non-linear. This illustration is complementary to that presented previously, in that these attitudes are formed *as responses to* the givens of existence.

The circle-graph included here delineates the world-view into themes that are represented by the assumptions and values one holds about oneself, others, the world, and the cosmos.

Assumptions and values about oneself would include those intentions to 'be' the qualities to which we aspire – to experience oneself as 'fair' or 'generous', for example, but also as an embodied self, which might

28 World-view

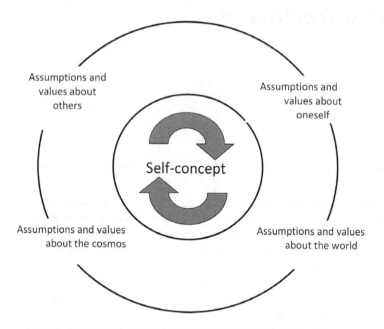

When aspects of the world-view are actualised, the self-concept (self-esteem) is positive. When aspects of the world-view are impeded from actualisation, the self-concept is threatened (self-esteem is diminished), often resulting in an antagonistic stance towards who or what is impeding the actualisation.

Figure 4.1 The world-view which is revealed through emotions
©Karen Weixel-Dixon 2011

include hopes for health or beauty. Assumptions and values about others are the expectations we have of how others should be and act, and this includes their behaviour towards us, especially their validation of the characteristics for which we wish to be acknowledged. Values and assumptions about the world are those that represent how we wish the world to be – the conditions of culture, society, and environment that we prize the most, and hope to assist in actualising. The values and assumptions about the cosmos approximate those of the 'Uberwelt' described earlier, in that these are the beliefs and meanings we ascribe to the universe at large, as demonstrated in convictions like 'everything happens for the best' or 'the universe has no regards for human affairs'.

In light of the anxiety that we endure with reference to uncertainty, contingency, and meaninglessness, it is understandable that such assumptions and values mitigate our discomfort by providing some sort of structure for us to carry out our day-to-day activities. It would be difficult to even make a seemingly modest decision without them; problems arise, however, when we fail to recall that these guiding principles are just that, and not absolute or permanent truths.

In a simplistic vignette, there may be the occasion when a pedestrian reaches a signposted crossing, but they hesitate to venture into the road if they suspect that the approaching vehicle is not aware of, or is choosing to ignore, their own right of way. At that moment, the person waiting to cross the route becomes aware that their assumption about what is 'expected' may not be shared by others, and if they are wise, they will hesitate at least long enough to verify if their expectations are correct. In such a moment, we may become sensitised to the possibility that what one holds as a value, an assumption, or an expectation is not, in that situation, shared or acted upon by others as anticipated. It may seem to be an innocuous scenario, but it can arouse the dormant dis-ease that attends the most basic anxiety provoked by the uncertainty of existence.

As is common in a dispute, parties believe that their own assumptions and expectations are the 'appropriate' ones, and that they are justifiably irate that the other side cannot agree with their perspective. Most often, the contestants find it difficult to believe that others might share the values that they themselves espouse, and deny the others' perspective any validity unless it coincides with the precise manner in which they themselves intend to have these principles realised.

For example, two families in dispute over a land parcel both hold similar family values: each side expects that others will and should respect the needs of households that support children and extended family members. Each side believes that these principles can be served only if the other parties will concede to the specifics of land ownership and management that they advocate; otherwise, the challengers are relegated to imposters, or worse.

In such an instance, even though the values may be common ground between the combatants, the practical implementation, that is, the actualisation of these aspects of the world-view, is impeded. Again, it can feel as if one's own 'being' is denied because one identifies oneself so closely with one's world-view.

The stakes are high in these brief scenarios: one's world-view is under scrutiny, if not threat, and the emotional response will probably be dramatic.

30 World-view

A serious challenge to one's world-view has an effect on one's self-concept. If aspects of the world-view are unacknowledged or obstructed, one may feel undermined, powerless, and ineffectual. Such a setback is yet another reminder that we are often at the mercy of people and circumstances over which we have little or no control, and of which we have but a meagre understanding.

The arrows at the centre of the drawing demonstrate that the self-concept is in flux. This is due in part to the effects of the process discussed above, and also to the constant dynamic of self as described previously. The self-concept is in an agreeable or acceptable state when the assumptions and expectations of the world-view are being implemented to at least some degree; the self-concept, however, is in a state of anxiety and high concern when the aspirations and assumptions are impeded or contested.

The heading of the representation of the world-view states that *emotions reveal* the world-view. Emotional reactions are the 'voices' that articulate the values that are implicated in any given situation; without the attending emotions, it would be much more difficult to ascertain what aspirations and expectations are being denied. Emotional expressions clearly indicate an *investment in the situation*; emotions are commensurate with the depth of one's care and interest. This is why they are a 'gift' to oneself as an involved party or as facilitator to a conflict resolution.

Much more will be said with respect to how to work with emotions as an aspect of exploration in a subsequent section of this text.

It is important to note that the world-view, as outlined here, provides a construct which may help us understand a person's 'private logic': their choices, intentions, and behaviours are all correlated with the values and assumptions attached to these categories. To the extent that we can appreciate the world-view, we will be able to comprehend the perspective of the person with whom we are engaged. One might say that there is no 'irrational' behaviour or perspective; such evaluations are reflections of an attempt to understand a person without reference to their own personal 'horizons'. One is reminded of the proverb: Those who dance are thought mad by those that hear not the music.

How we might achieve such insight will be a theme and a methodology explored under the topic of phenomenology.

The world-view of any individual, or group or dyad, provides only a 'snapshot' of their perspective: this perspective is, of course, impacted by a modified response to the 'givens'. As suggested in the vignette of the pedestrian crossing, our tightly held assumptions can sometimes become shaken, or 'de-sedimented'. On such occasions, we may subtly or radically modify our perspective. Every challenge to our assumptions and values necessitates a *new* choice, or *a re-choosing*.

Spinelli makes a significant contribution with respect to this mutability of the world-view when he employs the term 'worlding' in preference to language and models that seem to imply a static condition of living:

> When the structurally imposed restrictions upon 'constant becoming' are removed, the ever-shifting flux of being can be expressed in terms such as 'process-like' and 'action-based'. *Worlding . . .* is another, perhaps more adequate, term (Spinelli 2007, p. 20).

Although the term world-view will be employed in this text, the quality of changeability is retained in the description of human existence as invariably permeated by uncertainty, transience, change, choice, freedom, and meaninglessness; aligned with the proposal that the 'self' lacks an essence, and is a process-like dynamic, it may become more apparent that the self-concept, as well as all dimensions of the world-view, will be impacted by any modifications to any of the components.

Spinelli goes on to comment:

> the structural point of view we make of self, others, and the world in general is always incomplete . . . and hence, uncertain. Every moment of worlding is novel and unique, never to be repeated, never identical to any other. (ibid., p. 23)

As noted earlier, it is not just difficult to live without some structure, it is in fact impossible: the chaos and uncertainty at the heart of existence is 'de trop'.

This is a key principle in understanding that what makes choice so difficult, in those situations where it really matters, is that there are uncertain consequences, some of which may affect how others perceive me, how I perceive others, how I view the cosmos, and even how I conceive of myself. This is reflected in comments like 'This is so out of character her/him/them', or 'Now that I've said that, it doesn't really sound like me', or 'How can this happen?'

This inability to absolutely predict outcomes seemingly denies us the capacity to determine the 'right' choice ahead of time, that is, *the choice that will uphold our values and assumptions*. It is in this respect that Sartre proposed that we 'always make the right choice' (Sartre 1973): not the moral choice, but the one that we hope will most adequately realise our world-view. Again, we are reminded that our freedom is both a burden and a blessing; to deny this prerogative is a mode of inauthenticity.

32 World-view

This is *not* to say that adhering to one's values is necessarily a negative objective. However, it must be recognised that such a decision is a *new* choice, a re-choosing in a different time and context, even it if bears similarities in terms of rationale and strategies to previous occasions. Such is the effect of temporality and transience: we do not have the luxury of deciding something once and for all.

In a dispute, those involved are fighting to maintain their world-view in the face of challenges from others and in spite of misgivings that might be at the edge of awareness, even on those occasions in which the whole world stands in opposition to one's perspective. The prospect of entertaining change at this juncture seems to promise nothing but loss.

One of the fundamental assertions of this exposition is that it is far more effective to have some understanding of the problems and difficulties in any situation before considering how things might be different. Exploring the world-view held by anyone will serve this intention.

In support of this assertion, Spinelli comments:

> any therapeutic tampering with the presenting conflict without sufficiently understanding its relatedness to the client's world-view might well create far greater distress and unease in living than did the original presenting problem. (Spinelli 2007, p. 66)

In order to achieve even a modest understanding of another's world-view, we must facilitate an enquiry; this is in the hope of acknowledgement and discovery of what is at stake in a conflict.

The following discussions will hopefully clarify how this can best be accomplished, and how it may lead to a resolution that goes some way to satisfying the requirements of 'private logic'.

References

Deurzen-Smith, E. van 1988 *Existential Counselling in Practice*, Sage, London.
May, R. (1961) 1969 *Existential Psychology* (ed. R. May), McGraw-Hill, New York.
Sartre, J.P. (1948) 1973 *Existentialism and Humanism* (trans. P. Mairet), Methuen Publishing, London.
Spinelli, E. 2007 *Practising Existential Psychotherapy: The relational world*, Sage, London.
Strasser, F. and Randolph, P. 2004 *Mediation: A psychological insight into conflict resolution*, Continuum, London.

Chapter 5

Self and other

Both Heidegger and Sartre favour a view on existence, which is a state assigned only to humans, that posits the lack of *essence* in terms of what we are: there is no human nature, no 'self', in fact, as we are not-something, that is, *nothing*, to begin with; we form ourselves in our choices and actions.

'Existence precedes essence' is Sartre's assertion (Sartre 1973, p. 28), and Heidegger echoes: 'The "essence" of Dasein lies in its existence' (Heidegger 1993, p. 67).

And how might we understand the notion of 'existence'? Macquarrie refers to the etymology of the word to clarify the expression as it is employed in the literature:

> To 'exist' or 'ex-sist' (Latin: *ex-istere*) meant originally to 'stand out' or 'emerge'. . . . The verb had a more active *feel* about it . . . Putting it more philosophically, to exist is to stand out from nothing. (Macquarrie 1973, p. 62)

Human beings emerge or stand out by choosing which possibilities to realise, within their contextualised freedom, and in the actions they take to construct the world according to their values.

The implications of these tenets are dramatic and far reaching with respect to all the aspects of the human condition reviewed thus far; at this point, we can consider how they inform our understanding of self and Other.

These proposals reflect the employment of the word 'existence' as it was defined earlier: to emerge, to stand out. But these activities are not one-time events; they are a continuous unfolding, moving, dynamic. This process-like quality is comparable to the connotation of the term 'Dasein', employed by Heidegger to denote human being(s):

34 Self and other

it means "Being-there" . . . this noun Heidegger uses to designate us is the infinitive form of a *verb*. (Polt 1999, p. 30)

Again, we are reminded of the non-static quality of being, and of existing, for humans.

This may at first seem contradictory to the collection of conditions previously described as 'givens' of human existence. It should be emphasised that the givens are generalities, those universal elements assigned 'ontological' status, that is, *what* there is; ontological dimensions can tell us nothing about any given individual (or group). The specifics of *how* these are responded to are the 'ontic' manifestations. The ontic realm is where we discover *who and how* people are.

By virtue of this nothingness that is in us, that *is* us, we are able to say yes to some possibilities, and no to others: there is no determining factor, no essence that necessitates choosing one option over another.

These Western thinkers are not the only, or the first, philosophers to take this view on the non-existence of the self:

One would have to go to the East, to the Buddhist philosopher Nagarjuna (*circa* 200AD), with his doctrine of *Anatman*, the insubstantiality of the Self, to meet as awesome a list of negation as Sartre draws up . . . The Self . . . is in Sartre's treatment, as in Buddhism, a bubble, and a bubble has nothing at its center. (Barrett 1990, p. 247)

This necessity to actualise ourselves in our choices, again, provokes anxiety; all of the concerns that attend choosing to realise one possibility over another, and facing the responsibility of the consequences, are felt keenly, particularly when it involves *how we wish to be experienced* by others.

If I wish to be experienced as a reasonable and fair person, I will choose to behave in a manner that I hope will convey to others that I am characterised by these values. I may offer concessions in a disagreement, or I may go to some length to demonstrate that I embody these principles by presenting what seems to me to be an equitable resolution to a contest.

However, if the other party does *not* concur with, or, even worse, does not *believe* this self-concept that I am promoting, then there is likely to be a problem. In this scenario, it is not just my practical proposals that are rejected; it feels as if it is '*I*' who am denied.

We may recall that being-in-the-world-with-others has been designated as a given of human existence. What makes this problematic in a most crucial respect is that we need others to comprehend us, and appreciate us, as the *self* we aspire to be.

Sartre's (in)famous vignette known as 'the look' (Sartre 1993) is a dramatic illustration of this principle.

A man is caught peering through a keyhole. When he becomes aware that he is being surveilled, he experiences shame when subjected to the 'look' of the other person. In that moment, he realises that the other has judged him, and has totalised him as an undesirable character. The man under observation has no power to manage the observer's interpretation, even if he tried; the observer *may* alter his opinion, but that is at his discretion.

This process is fraught with complications. Even if I am confirmed by the other as I aspire to be, they have the prerogative to *change* their opinion; I am never completely safe from their characterisation of me. In this way, the other can impede my intentions to be acknowledged as the (self) person I wish to be; they pose a threat to *my freedom*, indefinitely.

This provides us with even deeper appreciation of how and why conflict is always personal, and is always taken personally.

This is evident in comments like 'Who do they take me for?' or 'They don't know who they're dealing with!' These expressions may seem like dramatic posturing, but they clearly illustrate that a large part of what is fuelling the fires is that the (other) combatant does not acknowledge or believe the self-concept that was initially being promoted by their opposition. The frustrated party therefore has to adopt an alternate behavioural strategy to impress the other side of their prowess, rather than their fair-mindedness, for example.

Although anyone may describe or evaluate another person in any given situation, this appraisal is not total or final, partly for reasons already noted—the other may change their opinion, or expand upon it. Also, however, being-in-the-world-with-others provides ample opportunity to be perceived and interpreted; *no one has the final say.*

With respect to conflict, and indeed, in all human engagements, it is important to recognise that the characterisation that has been described is in part *true* for this occasion of relatedness: if I am a party to a conflict, I can believe that the other may experience me as unfair, irrational, or even generous; whatever qualification is articulated has some merit with respect to the other's perspective at the time.

The impediment of one's attempts to be recognised and acknowledged as a person of particular attributes is fertile ground for conflict.

As might be inferred from the discussion so far, when an Other accords with one's own aspirations for a profile, for a self that is constituted by qualities that one cherishes, the resulting dynamic between the persons involved will approach that of kinship, if not love. This scenario

36 Self and other

promises *cooperation*, as those involved may collaborate in a project to value and support each other in their ambitions, and thereby their own as well.

Considering the arbitrary and dynamic nature of relationships in these respects, it is understandable that every human contact is likely to be tinged with uncertainty and anxiety. But one thing is clear: we exis*t in relation to other people* (Warnock 1992).

There are possibilities and liabilities in human relatedness. We can choose to respond to the issues correlated with relatedness in Bad Faith or in Good Faith, to use the Sartrean terms.

An example of Bad Faith in the context of relationships eschews shared responsibility for the quality of the relationship on the part of all those involved; this is a common scenario in marital contests. Each partner may blame the other totally for the condition of the relationship and the situation. The inverse of this process may be that *one* person may claim *all* the responsibility for the state of the relationship. In the former assertion, there is an attempt to avoid any responsibility; in the latter, there is an attempt to assume *all* responsibility, and thereby a positioning of oneself as the locus of control and power with reference to maintaining the status quo or implementing change.

In either case, it is an article of Bad Faith to ignore or evade the awareness that human relatedness is *co-constituted*; everyone in the dyad or the group shares the responsibility for the status of the relatedness, although not *necessarily* equally, or in the same manner.

Conducting a relationship in Good Faith would be to recognise that the other is complex and changeable, and responsible, in the same way that we all are. With such understanding, we might be more tolerant, if not appreciative, of the spontaneity in decisions and behaviour, and of the capacity for creative and experimental *response-ability.*

Our attempts to define each other, and ourselves, finally and totally, are meant to assuage the uncertainty and anxiety that is an inherent part of human relatedness.

Warnock notes:

> We wish people to conform to the descriptions we give of them. We wish to predict their behaviour entirely. (Warnock 1992, p. 16)

How much simpler life would be if this were so—but perhaps also a lot less interesting.

This ambition would apply to ourselves as well. If we could justify our choices on the basis that 'that's the kind of person I am', then all

Self and other **37**

would be forgiven, and no one should be disappointed, because one could not do otherwise. If 'I am what I am' holds true, then anyone who finds my behaviour unacceptable is holding unwarranted expectations.

As our existence is fundamentally relational, the other poses a threat to me in terms of how I wish to be seen as a person, even though this is only a 'snapshot' of how and who I am, as I continue to 'emerge'; and certainly other people can act either as a collaborator or an opponent in the actualisation of my hopes, ambitions, and intentions in the world at large.

The picture may seem gloomy, but, in fact, a conflict situation can be an opportunity to recognise one's aspirations and values, and to review the strategies that have been employed in the service of these intentions. Likewise, it can also be an occasion in which we come to appreciate the complexity of the person with whom we are so dramatically engaged, and come to recognise what is important and meaningful for them in this situation. Immediately, we can see that there is already common ground: both or all parties want or need something to happen, and find themselves obstructed by the other(s) involved. For any amount of satisfaction, we need the other's help.

In almost all conflict situations, the starting point is where all those involved are desperately trying to appear to be *invulnerable*, or at least less vulnerable, to the force or power of the opposition. This intention is ultimately divisive, and provokes posturing and threatening promises.

The initial position is one of demand: each side argues that their own priorities should take precedent over those of the opposition; righteousness, rationales, and imperatives are forcefully articulated. The theme, and the initial strategy, is one of domination. It is often at this juncture that the gulf between the contestants seems unbridgeable.

Whether one is a party to these events or seeking to facilitate a resolution, the goal is the same: to effect cooperation, at some level. The skills and strategies to promote such a movement will be elaborated in the second part of this text; for now, it can be understood in principle thus:

> In positive reciprocity, instead of manipulating or changing each other, we remain open to each other ... we are also able to be vulnerable and to *appeal* to each other for the *help* that we need. (Cannon and Lindberg 2013, p. 73)

Although this exposition is addressing life-partner relationships, the notion of collaboration is certainly apropos to the satisfaction that may be available to any of those embroiled in the conflict/resolution cycle.

38 Self and other

Hazel Barnes also discerns a hopeful mode of relating in Sartre's vignette of 'the look': the looked-at may look back at the observer. The quality of the 'regard' may alter:

> The Look may also be an exchange. And two people may look at the world together. (Barnes 1974, p. 64)

This may seem optimistic, but with respect to conflict, one must keep in mind that this hoped-for shift in perspective is in reference to the situation at hand specifically; we are not expecting a radical movement in the values held by those involved. However, that kind of meta-change can and does happen, as we shall see.

References

Barnes, H.E. 1974 *Sartre*, Quartet Books, London.

Barrett, W. (1962) 1990 *Irrational Man*, Anchor Books, New York.

Cannon, B. and Lindberg, R. 2013 'The Challenge of Being Yourself While Being Part of a Couple', in *Existential Perspectives on Relationship Therapy* (E. van Deurzen and S. Iacovou, eds.), Palgrave Macmillan, Basingstoke.

Heidegger, M. (1962) 1993 *Being and Time* (trans. J. Macquarrie and E. Robinson), Blackwell, Oxford.

Macquarrie, J. (1972) 1973 *Existentialism*, Penguin Books, London.

Polt, R. 1999 *Heidegger: An introduction*, UCL Press, London.

Sartre, J.P. (1948) 1973 *Existentialism and Humanism* (trans. P. Mairet), Methuen Publishing, London.

Warnock, M. (1970) 1992 *Existentialism*, Oxford University Press, Oxford.

Chapter 6

Time and temporality

Time matters to us. All cultures have mechanisms for notating and organising time, whether it is measured by mechanical timepieces or by natural events like the changing of the seasons. However, even without reference to any external indicators, we bear a relationship to time: we have a past, we have a future (until we don't), and we have a present that is elusive.

That human life is transient and finite, and that each of us knows this, grants us a special relationship with time that is not shared by objects or animals. Measured time, the object of scientific study, is somewhat different to temporality, which is a subjective phenomenon. Warnock puts it succinctly:

> Temporality is the name of the way in which time exists in human existence. (Warnock 1992, p. 62)

We assign the concepts of past, present, and future to our structure of time, and when we consider these aspects in greater depth, we can recognise conditions attached to each of these temporal elements: the past alerts us to the fact that we are 'thrown' into the world, born into circumstances over which we had no say or control; we are engaged with the immediate present; and the future holds the promise of as-yet-unfulfilled possibilities, including our death, the circumstances of which are unknown.

The time allotted to us is the ultimate limitation to all our possibilities, but it is not the only limitation. As suggested previously, our freedom is always situated: it is curtailed by conditions for which we are not responsible, like the particulars of our birth, our physiology, and our environment. Additionally, the choices we have made in the past, in the face of situated freedom, create new conditions: we may actualise new options

40 Time and temporality

with respect to particular issues, but our past remains unchanged. These immutable elements are known collectively as 'facticity'.

Additionally, time means transience: everything changes, human affairs all end. It has already been noted that change brings loss, and the necessity of making new decisions with respect to novel circumstances, possibilities, and new limitations. All of these conditions provoke anxiety, as they are correlated with uncertainty; we frequently cannot control *how* things change.

These qualities of temporality and time are so fundamental to the appreciation of what it means to be human that Heidegger deemed them constitutive properties of human existence ('Dasein' is Heidegger's term for human being):

> *Dasein itself . . .* is *time.* (Polt 1999, p. 96)

Temporality produces an effect that is particularly significant: it highlights the fact that we cannot postpone living, and that life matters to us. This realisation is designated as 'care' or 'concern'.

We cannot help but 'care'; our existence matters to us. Even when someone feigns indifference, it matters to them that they appear so; even when someone considers suicide, they do so because life matters to them in ways they find unbearable.

Care is manifest in our relation to death and to temporality, and is represented in the tension between the three aspects of time noted above. We have a past that *is already*, we have a future that holds possibilities, and we have a present that seems to demand our immediate attention, even as it passes into history.

These aspects of time, however, are coherent in a most crucial manner: one cannot be recognised without another. In the affairs of human beings, this trinity is perennially present with reference to choosing, willing, wishing, and acting.

Merleau-Ponty offers this insight:

> This moment of time calls all others to witness. (Merleau-Ponty 1999, p. 69)

When we consider a choice, we are limited by circumstances in our past (collectively and individually), and we are often haunted by possibilities that are now 'dead' to us. When we review our options, we are projecting ourselves into the future as we hope and intend it to be; these aspirations can inform the decisions we make as we attempt to actualise our intentions. In an effort to ascertain what is the *right* choice, we may obsessively review our past mistakes with the hope of not repeating them; this implies that we assume that historic circumstances are identical to those that we currently face.

When we become overwhelmed by the anxiety that our freedom and responsibility provoke, we may attempt to immerse ourselves in the present and strive to be content with the limbo that it appears to offer: the avoidance of choosing.

The latter situation is one that is marked as 'inauthentic': it is a delusion that provides some respite from the angst that attends the constant demands of agency and the quotidian threat of non-being. However, this comes at some cost: by allowing ourselves to become absorbed in the immediacy of our situation, we are prone to allocating our agency to external or communal sources in the attempt to avoid choosing or making a decision that will eliminate options; we seek to keep all our options 'alive'.

This strategy is also a delusion because it is impossible *not* to choose; to attempt to refrain from deciding is in itself a choice. Jean Paul Sartre characterises this attempt to deny our freedom as 'Bad Faith' (1993).

When we allow ourselves to become enthralled with the future, we deceive ourselves with the pretence that all things are possible; we act as if we stand in a world of unrestricted possibility. This can be manifested in extreme idealism, and the domination of fantasy in which actual engagement with choice is indefinitely postponed. This position too can lead to a case of inauthenticity:

> All genuine willing must take account of factical possibility. (Macquarrie 1973, p. 201)

If we do not recognise the limitations of our situated freedom, our decisions are based in illusion, and are doomed.

Immersion in the past, where there is a radical imbalance with the other temporal dimensions, can produce an infatuation with *what already is*, resulting in a 'stuckness' with reference to choosing and acting. The attitude is illustrated in the spurious query of 'What's the point?', or an extreme fascination with the particulars of historic events and projects. Such a narrow focus on the past can be an attempt to attenuate the anxiety that attends freedom, choice, and uncertainty.

It is apparent that all three aspects of time are operating collectively and simultaneously.

Upon review of these principles, one might infer that there is an emphasis on one of these temporal dimensions: that of the future. This is

42 Time and temporality

primarily a Heideggerian (1993) view, and one worth considering with respect to the topic of conflict.

Weixel-Dixon and Strasser note:

> In part, 'care' indicates an orientation towards the future, towards the ultimate eventuality and possibility of our demise . . . Care is a pro-ject towards death. (Weixel-Dixon and Strasser 2005, p. 230)

In short, we are beings-toward-death, and for Heidegger, and others, this is the inevitable focus for our life projects, and has the greatest impact on our decisions. We summon our past experiences to inform us on how to choose for the uncertain future; we take action and we adopt behaviour that we hope or assume will support the implementation of our intentions.

In a conflict, the contestants often wish to review the past to understand more fully the losses that are implicated. They want their current discomfort to be attenuated, and by virtue of the historical focus, they are frequently distracted from the possibilities, as yet unimagined, that could serve their interests in some way or to some extent.

Even in this over-simplified equation, it is apparent that *it is the future-becoming-present that holds the promise of some gratification.*

These premises will be expanded upon when we consider the strategies for facilitating a resolution to a dispute.

However, there are a few correlated proposals that are to be addressed if we wish to more fully understand these observations in relation to conflict.

As has been suggested, if we refuse to acknowledge our freedom, which is coincidental to choice, possibility, and limitations, we stand in inauthenticity; that is, we divert our attention away from the givens by virtue of excuses, and various other methods that are employed in an effort to abdicate our responsibility and refute our facticity. It may be understood, then, that standing in *authenticity* requires us to squarely face these issues, and adopt a *stance* towards them; it is here that our freedom is exercised.

The benefit of such a response is that we become the authors of our own existence. This is not to say that we are in control of what happens to us, but rather that we have some latitude, even in the direst circumstances, to respond to our situation. The response(s) we adopt do not preclude suffering; it allows us to choose the value for which we are prepared to suffer. It is often the case that we endure discomfort, but we retain the moral high ground, as the chosen option represents a principle in which we are invested.

At this juncture, it is important to note a certain caveat: authenticity is not held as a 'norm' in existential psychotherapy, or indeed in conflict. It is a possible 'state of being' (Cohn 2002), and, as is the case with all polarities, necessitates the opposite state of being, or mode of existing.

The relevance for conflict may now become clearer: it is critical to discover and acknowledge *how* those involved regard their positions in terms of their own choice, responsibility, and possibilities. This interest will frequently be considered throughout this exposition.

It must also be highlighted that *loss*, particularly the loss of a future to which we aspire, and for which we have struggled and now feel entitled to, is the crux of much of our suffering, and certainly a key issue in relation to dispute: if someone else is implicated in provoking such a loss, they will be viewed as an appropriate source for redress by the injured party.

This is a crucial aspect with reference to the givens of temporality and responsibility as it relates to life, and particularly to disputes. If an individual, or a group, stands to incur a significant loss, it is preferable to assign the accountability for this effect to another party; this vindicates the person who is deemed to be the victim of *someone else's* malfeasance or bad judgement. In this way, the person acquitted of any responsibility can *maintain* their confidence with respect to future choices and decisions, and they can be liberated from any guilt that they may have harboured.

In contradiction to what the opposition has probably implied, the complainant avoids being characterised as the source of their own misery. If someone else is to blame, according to the perspective held by the injured party, then that culprit must admit their liability and offer some kind of compensation.

Such a position may appear as radically black or white. We prefer absolutes, and the clarity and simplicity they provide. It can be noted, however, that blame is in the service of a defence against the messier, more complicated scenario: it is possible, if not likely, that we each contribute in some way to our own suffering, and to the many disagreements in which we become entangled.

Time and temporality permeate all aspects of human existence. They remind of us our impotence in terms of finitude, and the ultimate possibility and eventuality. In an effort to alleviate the attendant anxiety of these conditions, we subscribe to illusions like 'I can do anything if I really put my mind to it' or 'Thinking positive will make it so'. However, as Becker has asserted (1976), our anxieties also move us to create culture, society, and family in the hopes of transcending these mortal restrictions. There is a gain and a loss to everything, and certainly the same can be said for our responses to the human predicament.

References

Becker, E. (1975) 1976 *Escape from Evil*, Free Press, New York.

Cohn, H.W. 2002 *Heidegger and the Roots of Existential Therapy*, Continuum, London.

Macquarrie, J. (1972) 1973 *Existentialism*, Penguin Books, London.

Merleau-Ponty, M. (1962) 1999 *Phenomenology of Perception* (trans. Colin Smith), Routledge, London.

Polt, R. 1999 *Heidegger: An introduction*, UCL Press, London.

Sartre, J.P. (1943) 1993 *Being and Nothingness* (trans. H.E. Barnes), Routledge, London.

Weixel-Dixon, K. and Strasser, F. 2005 'Time and Purpose', in *Existential Perspectives on Human Issues* (E. van Deurzen and C. Arnold-Baker, eds.), Palgrave Macmillan, Basingstoke.

Chapter 7

The contributions of phenomenology

Phenomenology is a philosophy that is concerned with how we, as conscious beings, come to know 'reality'.

We perceive our surroundings, our reality, even ourselves, and we attempt to understand them, to make 'sense' of these phenomena. *How* this transpires is the subject of this philosophical approach.

This branch of philosophy had its modern origins in Continental European thinkers and writers who shared an interest in the structure and function of consciousness with reference to how 'objects are experienced and present themselves to our consciousness' (Spinelli 1989, p. 2). These include psychic phenomena, like ideas, as well as other beings like ourselves. They originally hoped to discover a method or a means by which reality could be revealed in all its raw, unadulterated essence, without being tainted by the assumptions and interpretations applied by consciousness.

Underlying this ambition is the assumption that it is both desirable and possible to 'know' what is objectively real. Perhaps even this enterprise was a means of engaging with the uncertainty and contingency that permeates existence.

It is beyond the scope of this text to review in detail the origins and development of this approach. In support of the aim of this discussion, the focus here will be on that perspective generally recognised as existential phenomenology.

When we *perceive* anything, we perform an invariable mental act: we interpret what meets us; we assess it for value, meaning, threat, comfort, security, etc. And, as human existence is described as being-in-the-world, we cannot have an 'objective' view on what we perceive: we are bound to it, bound up in it; we are in the midst of it. Our perception is entangled in reality, and the experience of what meets us is affected by, and permeated with, our vantage point. This dynamic is a function of consciousness.

46 Contributions of phenomenology

Phenomenologists, although varied in the specifics of their approach, concur in their description of the structure of consciousness and its effects: this structure, or process, is known as 'intentionality'.

There are two focal points in this structure: the noema, or *what* it is we are perceiving or aware of, and noesis, the manner in which we experience the what, that is, the *how* of one's experience (Ihde 1986, Langdridge 2007, Spinelli 1989).

There is a further implication to this proposal: we don't just perceive, we *re-perceive*, and with every passing moment, and with every (even slight) inevitable change in the world which we perceive, our interpretation of what meets us *may* be modified. In perceiving new data or information, we encounter a novel horizon: our interpretation of the elements of that horizon may be adjusted. Whether we *allow* such a modification will be considered further; however, it is apparent that it is *possible* to make such alterations, and this is evidenced in everyday life. An example of this would be that an event in the past, which at that time might have been endured as a disastrous occurrence, is at a later date re-appraised and viewed instead as a blessing.

It is important to recall that what meets us includes the assumptions and expectations that currently underpin our world-view, as well as other entities and objects. These can all occupy the 'what' focal point of our perception.

When we are aware that our world-view is open to re-interpretation by virtue of our own freedom, we may experience the 'dizziness' of freedom (Kierkegaard 1980) that can de-stabilise any pretensions to absolute truth or certainty. Our assumptions are disclosed in all their contingency; that is, the 'how' of our conscious process that assigns meaning to our experiences is fundamentally flexible.

It becomes evident that each of us construes our experience of the world. It is also apparent that others are doing the same, and this is the source of the inexhaustible possibilities for differing, if sometimes similar, perspectives, expectations, and assumptions between and amongst people, even when this involves the same 'facts' or circumstances.

The significance of this for interpersonal conflict may be appreciated in that whether one is a party to a conflict or is attempting to mediate a dispute, there is no final or absolute 'truth' with reference to the situation: the 'facts' are interpreted by all involved, and the perspectives that emerge are amenable to re-interpretation, even if, at certain junctures, those involved may not seem inclined to see it this way. Additionally, the facilitator to any such contentious engagement must also understand that they too are subject to their own biases and particular perspectives,

Contributions of phenomenology 47

and that what limited understandings they have of any given situation are subject to modification, and represent an evolving comprehension.

We are reminded, as suggested previously, that change is a constant of human existence.

We will consider the practicalities of how and why perspectives may be modified, and also why there may be some resistance to any alteration of one's initial understanding of a situation or an experience.

Although the ambition set out by early phenomenologists to discover 'things in themselves' (Husserl 1970) was never realised, a method evolved for granting a more adequate, and more complex, appreciation of the objects and entities that we encounter in the world. This is known as the phenomenological method of investigation (Ihde 1986, Langdridge 2007, Spinelli 1989).

In the format that is most relevant to existential therapy, the phenomenological method comprises four basic 'rules' (Langdridge 2007, Spinelli 1989). These rules grant us an understanding of what part we play in construing our 'reality'.

The first is the rule of 'epoché'. In the attempt to set aside our judgements and opinions of what we experience, the 'how' of our experience, we may come to appreciate more deeply and fully the 'what' of our experience. The aim is to recognise and acknowledge our assumptions, and to bracket them, or suspend them, as much as possible in order to see something or someone in a 'fresh' light.

Having accomplished this naive stance to some degree, we are encouraged to eschew our usual explanations for what we are experiencing, and to seek only to *describe* what we are immediately experiencing. The longer this descriptive process is allowed to continue, the more likely it is that we will discover aspects in our descriptions that previously went unnoticed. This new information may have an impact on how we then evaluate the experience of objects, events, or people.

Although we must eventually produce some theories and explanations of our experience in order to act upon the world, these too often become conclusions that are rarely reconsidered, until we find it useful or necessary to reflect upon them.

A third step is to 'horizontalize', that is, to forego placing a hierarchy of value or significance on any of the elements of the experience we have described. Again, this is in an effort to 'make room' for a more complex understanding of what it is we are conscious of.

Once this method has been deployed, we can then consider whether, or to what extent, our original hypotheses and assumptions were appropriate, or if they warrant further consideration or modification.

48 Contributions of phenomenology

This process can provide a very effective means of exploring one's experience. If one takes the time to consider what assumptions and prejudices might be at play in terms of how one evaluates the current situation, the present encounter, or the idea that is being entertained, a novel or an extended perspective might become apparent.

An example of this might be the male partner in a heterosexual couple who expresses his expectation that a female mediator will favour the woman partner and will therefore attempt to influence the process based on her bias. When the husband's assumption is not validated, he may either reconsider his viewpoint or appreciate that he is mistaken, at least on this occasion, or he may construct a theory that allows him to maintain his perspective: he may claim that this particular female mediator is envious of her female client, and that she consequently harbours a preference for the position of the husband.

If the possibility of being mistaken in one's assumptions is entertained, a shift in some aspect of the world-view is likely to occur; this in turn is likely to affect the other dimensions of the world-view: the aspects of self, others, the world, and the cosmos. Such changes can be challenging, as they indicate that our existence is permeated with chaos.

If one refuses to recognise that one's expectations and values are tenuous and contingent, then one is forced to deny the novel information that a revised assumption might provide. People seek certainty and confirmation in an effort to cope with the uncertainty that is an inherent condition of life.

To change, or even modify, one's world-view, requires a new choice. When we engage with this choosing, we are reminded that we are responsible, and that we base our decisions on the very limited information that we possess, and that this information is itself often sourced in changeable propositions.

Applying the phenomenological method can be invaluable in terms of understanding our experiences of ourselves, of others, and certainly of disputes. Conflict, to a large extent, is a consequence of mistaken assumptions, unacknowledged biases, the lack of recognition of possibilities, and the denial of common ground between the factions. If the process described above was deployed more frequently, it could provide fresh perspectives on any of our experiences, allowing us a greater scope for choice and action.

However, this is not to suggest that this is a method to recommend to parties of a dispute. It is a reflective practice that can benefit those involved in a dispute, either as parties to the contest or as mediators or facilitators for a resolution. It is also a useful tool for considering our own perspective on conflict in general: Is conflict seen as simply a challenge

Contributions of phenomenology 49

to our own world-view, which is to be defended at any cost? Or can it be viewed as an opportunity to expand our understanding of the compelling situation, and thereby of ourselves and others?

The principles described above serve as reminders that with reference to human affairs, 'truth' and 'reality' are constructs that are subject to re-interpretation. They are malleable, and basically lack permanence or absolute certainty.

This aspect of uncertainty and contingency was discussed earlier when it was recognised as a given of human existence. As we cannot tolerate a constant state of uncertainty, we create (or adopt, which is also a choice) assumptions, values, and expectations as guiding principles for choice and action. These are the elements that constitute our world-view. These are responses to the conditions of human existence, and it is these that are subject to revision as we discover new possibilities and horizons.

But the essential plasticity of our guiding principles can exacerbate our anxiety. We would often prefer to have absolutes, definitive truths and perspectives that would relieve us of the responsibility for choosing, and provide indisputable rationales for our decisions. So in an effort to buffer ourselves from the burden of responsibility that is concomitant with freedom, we refuse novel perspectives, and we abjure possibilities that might necessitate a modification to our world-view. That is, we go on the defensive.

When the assumptions of our world-view are challenged, we can employ a descriptive investigation – as described in the phenomenological method – in an effort to allow for other possibilities of perception and response, thereby reminding ourselves, as well as demonstrating to others, that we are aware that there is more than one truth, even more than one *kind* of truth. Or, in a bid for righteousness and safety from the possibility of being mistaken, which would demand that we engage with uncertainty, we mount a counter-offensive.

It is this defence against the possibility for change in our evaluations and perspectives that is the impediment to really listening to the views and intentions of others. If we 'hear' and understand the world-view of someone else, we may not be able to maintain our own position; we may be affected by their rationale and perspective, and may recognise that our own is limited only by our own interests.

References

Husserl, E. (1900) 1970 *Logical Investigations* (trans. J.N. Findlay), Humanities Press, New York.

50 Contributions of phenomenology

Ihde, D. (1977) 1986 *Experimental Phenomenology: An introduction*, Albany State University, New York.

Kierkegaard, S. (1844) 1980 *The Concept of Anxiety* (trans. R. Thomte), Princeton University Pess, Princeton, NJ.

Langdridge, D. 2007 *Phenomenological Psychology: Theory, research and method*, Pearson/Prentice Hall, Harlow, England.

Spinelli, E. 1989 *The Interpreted World: An introduction to phenomenological psychology*, Sage, London.

Chapter 8

The contributions of hermeneutics

There are common themes that are central to the subjects of phenomenology and hermeneutics. Truth, knowledge, and understanding are shared core concerns in these philosophical inquiries.

Cohn offers this etymology of the philosophical title:

> 'Hermeneutics' is derived from the Greek verb 'hermeneuien' (to interpret), and it is important to remember that it refers us to Hermes, the divine messenger god of the ancient Greeks. (Cohn 2005, p. 221)

The deification of the messenger implies that what we are about to hear or read demands our attention, and that the message will most likely request, if not require, a response.

Originally the term 'hermeneutics' referred to an interpretation of religious texts, but it has more recently been applied not only to a variety of written materials, but also to narratives, to language, and to human existence as it is expressed in these mediums.

As with phenomenology, it would be impossible to do justice to the various thinkers and authors who have contributed to this philosophical approach. What will be reviewed here are those proposals that have import for the project of understanding and working with conflict. Some of these tenets are sourced in the works of Martin Heidegger, Wilhelm Dilthey, Friedrich Schleiermacher, and Hans-Georg Gadamer. Additionally, there will be a number of references to psychotherapeutic practitioners who appreciate the relevance of hermeneutics for their work.

It has been proposed previously in the section on phenomenology that our engagement with the world and everything in it, including ourselves,

52 Contributions of hermeneutics

others, and psychic phenomena like ideas and assumptions, is subject to interpretation. With everything that we perceive, we invariably assign it meaning and significance.

Interpretation is necessary when we do not understand something, something that is foreign or at least unfamiliar. However, in order to even begin to interpret, we summon all that we might already recognise, even vaguely, about the phenomenon we encounter; interpretation then becomes a composite of the known and the unknown, and the understanding thus acquired will be limited and enhanced by these factors. This process is, in fact, ongoing; with every novel element of understanding, be it of an object or a person, we have a new perspective, and we have new 'knowledge' that can then be brought to bear on the next interpretation. This dynamic is commonly known as the 'hermeneutic circle'.

The circular reference yields significant implications: no interpretation, no understanding, is ever complete or total; something always remains to be discovered.

These interpretations are in the service of understanding. We want to know about others and objects and events; we *need* to know, one might say, because sometimes our very existence depends upon it. However, our desire to know is also predicated on our intolerance of uncertainty. We would hope to obtain knowledge that makes life and relationships less risky, less contingent, and more predictable, to the point where we no longer are encumbered with the responsibility of choosing on the basis of incomplete or changeable information.

The quality of the kind of interpretation that is elucidated in philosophical and existential literature is hermeneutical, as opposed to reductive. A most common example of the reductive interpretation is that of the psychoanalytical model, in which the analyst does the interpreting *for* the patient, as the patient is not able to 'objectively' recognise their situation; one can also note this kind of interpretation in scientific paradigms where everything is recorded by a detached observer and reduced to a simplistic model, as in causality. These kinds of interpretations serve as explanations and conclusions. They may provide a satisfying finality to a practical query and relieve the inquisitor of any further involvement or responsibility.

In contrast, in an existential hermeneutic project, the listener will seek to assist the speaker in the 'unfolding' of the meanings that are being explored, in a participatory manner, as a joint venture. The significance of the interpretation is relative and inter-subjective; a certain naiveté on the part of the listener is desirable.

Contributions of hermeneutics   53

However, where there is a possibility of even limited understanding, there is also the possibility of mis-understanding: only further experience, review, and re-interpretation can yield a more adequate insight.

And this brings us to an understanding of what is deemed by existential thinkers to be the most profound form of knowing, that is, knowing that is gained from inter-relational, inter-subjective encounters. This position is not to denigrate the kind of knowing that is pursued in scientific projects: an accumulation and analysis of facts as they are collected by a detached observer. It is rather to place a particular value on the meanings that come to light in mutuality and reciprocity; this is the kind of knowing that is relevant to the appreciation of persons, of their perspectives, and of their world-views. It is to encounter an Other, and to enter into dialogue with an Other, in the hopes of meeting them, as well as oneself, on the road to understanding.

The context in which these interpretations and inquiries of meaning is most effectively conducted is referred to as a 'dialogical attitude' (Spinelli 2007).

Dialogue is produced in language, but it is also an *attitude* about how a conversation takes place that distinguishes it from how we conduct everyday conversations. In a dialogical attitude, the communication is fluid, though not always comfortable, and the flow of the talk is seemingly without agenda, other than to be understood by those involved. This seemingly aimless and creative character of such speech is aptly described by Gadamer:

> The more language is a living operation, the less we are aware of it. (Gadamer 2008, p. 65)

When a dialogue is occurring, the meanings and truths of the speech are unfettered, freed from guided direction and specific intent other than understanding, which is different to but not exclusive of the practicality of comprehension. It is spontaneous, creative, and thereby largely unpredictable. Vedder, referencing Friedrich Schleiermacher's hermeneutics, comments on this quality:

> conversation is only meaningful if the ideal of complete knowledge remains unattainable. (Vedder 1999, p. 420)

The implication of this description is that dialogue necessitates a certain quality of 'being-with'—to be involved, to participate, and to thereby to be *affected*—because dialogue is experiential, not just an intellectual exercise.

54 Contributions of hermeneutics

Gadamer suggests:

> A second feature of the being of language is its I-lessness . . . speaking does not belong in the sphere of the 'I' but in the sphere of the 'We'. (Gadamer 2008, p. 65)

Additionally, the meanings and interpretations that were discovered and revealed are not 'completed' either; they stand as works in progress, subject to review in the next dialogical engagement.

We are reminded of previous proposals that characterised 'truth' as a contingent and inter-relational perspective. The same can be said of 'understanding'.

However, this project has consequences. The quality of such participation is likely to be revelatory for all concerned. It is the occasion of shared horizons, of a deep appreciation of, though not necessarily agreement with, another person's perspective. This is the possibility and source of empathy, or *resonance*; we don't look *at* the person we are engaged with as if they were an object of study, but rather we look *with* them, standing alongside them in the attempt to share their horizon, their perspective on *how* they are experiencing something, and what they wish to communicate.

But in acquiring this depth of understanding, one may be exposed to the arbitrary nature of one's own position: it could all be otherwise. Gadamer comments on this effect of true dialogue:

> It is true of every conversation that through it something different has come to be. (Gadamer 2008, p. xxii)

And here we can see the source of change: new understandings and new perspectives can provide more, and novel, options.

In this review of some of the principles of hermeneutics, we are considering how to facilitate understanding and change. In this dialogical project, one's views can be explored, *unfolded*, expanded. Any of those involved in this process can be freed from simply and vehemently defending their position, and can become aware that there are many, and often competing, aspects of their world-view, that is, their own values, that they are trying to serve in any given situation.

What makes this kind of communication effective, and affective, is also what can cast it as threatening: new understanding almost *necessitates* change, and, again, such modifications are not wholly predictable. Additionally, there is a possible liability in being understood: one's vulnerabilities can be exposed and exploited.

Contributions of hermeneutics   55

And these concerns are the principle reasons why people involved in a dispute are dis-inclined to *listen in order to understand* the other side. They may be listening for material to bolster their position, or information to exploit their opponent's weaknesses, but the anxiety evoked by the possibility of change can dispose anyone to deny or avoid any possibility for modification of their own perspective. As noted previously, any challenge to any aspect of the world-view can have far-reaching consequences for all of the concomitant assumptions and aspirations. Even if this possibility isn't fully comprehended, it has been experienced.

It should be noted that it is not possible to 'manufacture', or to summon, the kind of presence that has been described here as the dialogical attitude; one must be available for it, and maintain hope that an Other will engage in kind. However, the quality of such presence is not all or nothing; there are possibilities for such encounters in many conditions of communication, as there are many levels of understanding and connection.

So why would anyone take the risk of opening themselves to such a possibly profound and uncomfortable situation as the encounter described here?

Via the communication that is associated with dialogical presence, one can recognise that a change of intention, with respect to new understandings, can *perhaps* better serve the realisation of one's values and expectations, although not without some loss. It is inevitable that when one says 'yes' to something, one also says 'no' to something else; we cannot have it all. But novel understandings give greater latitude in exercising one's freedom to choose. In many cases, this is a choice with respect to what we are willing to give up in order to actualise another option. So, there is hope that in entering into such communication as described here, one may mitigate loss, and improve the chances of achieving some purpose.

The significance and value of the dialogical and hermeneutic principles espoused here is that they serve as a foundation for the understanding of, and subsequent resolution for, any dispute. In acquiring a more intricate and comprehensive appreciation of one's aspirations and values, and/or those of another, the options for actualising at least some of these multiply; there is at least hope that *all* will not be lost. Additionally, in keeping with the statement that 'it is always personal', the resolution will be deeply personal and relevant.

In the following sections of this book, we will explore skills that flow from this kind of engagement, as well as strategies that are the fruit of these more complex understandings. However, it is necessary that the

56 Contributions of hermeneutics

proposals that underpin interpretation and dialogue are appreciated; if not, then the inquiries and explorations that are essential for facilitating conflict resolution may become tools of coercion and bias.

References

Cohn, H.W. 2005 'Interpretation: Explanation or understanding?', in *Existential Perspectives on Human Issues* (E. van Deurzen and C. Arnold-Baker, eds.), Palgrave Macmillan, Hampshire, UK.

Gadamer, H.-G. (1976) 2008 *Philosophical Hermeneutics* (trans. D.E. Linge), University of California Press, Los Angeles.

Spinelli, E. 2007 *Practising Existential Psychotherapy: The relational world*, Sage, London.

Vedder, B. (1998) 1999 'Schleiermacher', in *A Companion to Continental Philosophy* (S. Critchley and W.R. Schroeder, eds.), Blackwell, Oxford.

Part I summary

The delineation of the givens of existence that are explored here is not comprehensive, nor do all philosophers and practitioners agree on these conditions; however, those presented here are aspects of existence that have particular relevance to conflict situations.

These universal concerns grant us common ground; we have a route to some fundamental understanding of what it is to be human. The commonality of these issues promises 'resonance', a possibility of being alongside an Other in order to share their view on the world to some degree. This comprehension can be deepened in dialogue—reciprocal communication that is in the service of clarifying and revealing the world-views of those involved. Such being-with requires courage; in being understood, we expose our vulnerabilities, and can also be affected in a manner that may move us to modify our perspectives.

The world-view is the seat of private logic. Here we can see how each of us engages with the universal aspects, thereby giving us some source, some rationale, for our choices and decisions. The world-view comprises our assumptions, expectations, and aspirations for ourselves (our self-concept), others, the world, and the cosmos.

However, it is essential to note that the world-view is, at any given moment, just a 'snapshot' of how we develop and evolve our interaction with, and reaction to, the givens. It is in this exercise of our freedom that we have the greatest latitude for change and growth; we can moderate our attitude towards the things that are inevitable. As the aspects of the world-view are all interconnected and interdependent, where there is an alteration in any of the categories, there is a shift in all.

And, with every choice, we have consequences, many of which are undesirable and unexpected. We may recognise the limits of our power to create our future as we would hope it to be.

58 Part I summary

Our awareness of possibilities, for better or worse, imbues our existence with uncertainty. The agency we so treasure comes with liabilities, as we accrue experiences that demonstrate that it is not possible to 'know' what is the right choice. Additionally, our evaluations of our previous actions may change, according to the outcomes. This changeability applies also to our relationships; no amount of contracts or promises can guarantee the constancy of anyone's sentiments.

Even though each of us is burdened and blessed with freedom, albeit contextualised, we fall short of possessing the power to *actualise* many of our ambitions independent of the collaboration of others. This is the source of conflict, of compromise, of love and hate in all its forms. To the extent that we are aided by another, we have positive affections; to the extent that the other person impedes our efforts, we have problematic, if not debilitating, relations. This is a significant aspect with respect to self-and-other: we need each other to substantiate how we wish to be perceived and experienced; we also need others to help us establish what we value in terms of actualities in the world. These ambitions are at the core of all relationships, friendly or combative.

One's world-view is often representative of one's personal 'truths'; however, the proposals of hermeneutic and phenomenological philosophies remind us that these 'truths' are malleable and subjective.

Phenomenology also proposes a 'method' of enquiry, or a stance that is often described as an 'attitude'. This attitude seeks to reach the 'things in themselves', which remains as an aspiration, as this is not a possibility for a subject who is immersed in what they are purporting to objectively observe (Heidegger 1993). However, this method, described previously in greater detail, allows for a more adequate appreciation of our experiences, including our perceptions of others.

These perspectives on truth and reality allow for an exploration that is based on a certain 'naiveté', in which those involved review and reconsider their perspectives with a less biased attitude; this in turn promotes a modified 'horizon', a position that opens up different possibilities.

As is often the case in disputes, each person has their own 'truth', represented by their version of the 'facts'. It is this version, this interpretation, of the facts that can reveal what values are being contested in any given dispute. It must be recognised, however, that people may cling to a fixed truth, because to entertain another perspective may have serious consequences for the credibility of their world-view. To acknowledge, even privately, that one is mistaken in any degree is to become entangled with uncertainty.

Time, or temporality as it is referred to in many expositions, is always an important factor in disputes, and in life. Time marks change, and change can bring loss. Some of these losses are the result of forces beyond our control, and some are the consequence of our own decisions and actions.

The defence against loss is a key factor in disputes. We strive to mitigate pending losses, in terms of our hopes and aspirations; we attempt to ward off further loss by inspecting the past for clues as to how to avoid making similar mistakes of judgement.

Temporality also implies finitude and death. The issue of death refers to more than one's demise, or that of a loved one; it also signals the death of opportunities, and the limitations inherent in mortality.

Time spent can never be regained. This provides a great motivational force with regard to bringing difficult situations, and the suffering endured, to a close. There is no guarantee that the suffering will end; sometimes the choice left to one is to choose between different kinds of suffering.

Such factors are all relevant to conflict, and the possibilities for resolution. All disputes come to an end of some kind—defeat, surrender, compromise—and then the cycle of dispute and resolution continues. The hope is that the outcome of a dispute can produce a collaboration that strengthens relationships rather than destroy them.

Reference

Heidegger, M. (1962) 1993 *Being and Time* (trans. J. Macquarrie and E. Robinson), Blackwell, Oxford.

Case vignette 1

The family

'How dare you!' Mrs. H shouted. Though her voice didn't carry much volume, the indignation was apparent.

'Martha, come on, the boy is suffering already ... please, let's see if we can work something out ...' Mr. H was attempting to be placatory, but he was flushed and sitting with his back pushed into the sofa cushions.

Max was pale, but sneering openly at his mother's outrage. He had accused her of 'faking a "good" marriage' and of pretending to be 'holier than thou' in reference to his own behaviour.

There was a pause in what was a stormy joint meeting. I waited to see if there was more, or if they would repeat the accusations that had been produced already.

'Max', began Mr. H, 'your behaviour is having serious effects on your mother and I ... and it has also nearly destroyed your own family ... what do you think ...' He paused. 'What do you think would help?'

'Oh please!' Mrs H commented with obvious exasperation. 'We've tried everything; every expert in the field of addiction has been consulted ... Max has seen everyone in the county, and at our expense. In spite of what he says now, we are trying; we have been there for him ... where does it end? No wonder his wife won't have him back; he hasn't really grown up.'

At least they were talking to each other, not just to me; I took that as a good sign. They were trying to communicate, even if the messages were unpalatable at the moment. I also noted that it seemed that Mr. and Ms. H spoke to, and about, Max as if he were an adolescent. He was, in fact, a man in his thirties with a family of his own. This latter observation I set aside, as it was not an appropriate challenge at the moment.

62 Case vignette: The family

'You should know, Mother . . . after all, addiction runs in families . . . and, apparently, lots of other shitty habits!' Max looked confident, and indeed, from Mrs. H's face, I could see he had struck a nerve.

'Enough Max! Doesn't family mean anything to you? Are you so prepared to give up on your own?' Mr. H extended both hands, palms up, in a gentle entreaty.

They had each given a brief synopsis of how they saw the current situation at the beginning of our joint meeting; it was all very civilised at first. It was an improvement to hear and see where the hurt lay, and where there was investment, which was clearly evident in the emotional expressions.

I decided to move ahead with the private sessions; this format had been decided prior to the joint session. It was agreed that I would see Max first, then Mr. and Mrs. H together. I made it clear that we could reconvene for another joint meeting at some point, if that was acceptable to all.

I was aware of the background to the dispute via the referral from the family's doctor. Max, thirty-two years of age, was married with two children, and he had been an alcoholic for most of his adult life. He had lost his job two years prior to our meeting, at which point his wife had kicked him out, and he had recently asked for, and been granted, shelter with his parents. It was known that he had been living on the streets for the last year. He hadn't seen or contacted his family during that time, but he had been notified by a friend that they were being supported by his in-laws, who were wealthy professionals.

Mr. and Mrs. H were in their early sixties and had a comfortable life after working for some years in the modest manufacturing business they had started. They now enjoyed semi-retirement. They had been aware of Max's problem with alcohol, but had hoped that settling into his own family life would have a stabilising effect on him; instead, his drinking became worse, he had abandoned his family, and they were 'deprived' of seeing their grandchildren, as their daughter-in-law seemed to blame them for Max's condition.

Max was currently residing with his parents, but there had been innumerable scenes, both at home and in public, in which he had been extremely drunk, sometimes aggressive, and generally antagonistic. His parents did not agree between them on what was an appropriate stand: Mr. H wanted Max to remain with them until he could 'take care of himself and his family', and Mrs. H wanted Max out, even if they had to rent him an apartment, as she felt this was the means to force him to re-assume his responsibilities.

Case vignette: The family 63

I showed Mr. and Mrs. H to their own room, where they could help themselves to refreshments, and explained that I would return to see them after my session with Max.

When I returned to the office, Max was sitting calmly, looking through messages on his phone.

'So, what are your thoughts about the situation, Max?' I wanted him to discuss what was most important for him to communicate.

'They owe it to me; they are still my parents, after all! They talk about being responsible; what crap! They have responsibilities towards me; they can't just stop being parents!' He banged his knee with the cell phone before stuffing it in his pocket.

He looked at me to see if I was in any way agreeing with him. I remained thoughtful.

'I know about this, at least, because I am a parent too . . . it never f***ing ends . . . it never stops . . . and it is really f***ing hard, most of the time. I'm not cut out for it; I wish I was . . .' Max rubbed his head with both hands and dropped them into his lap with some force.

'Do you have children?' he demanded.

'No—no, I don't.' I paused. I thought he might elaborate on his query, but I didn't feel this was the time to probe for the significance of the information I had given; if it was important, it would probably come up again.

'What's it been like for you, as a parent, and now as a child of adult parents?' Although this question was related to his last comment, I wasn't certain it was the most inviting probe, but I decided I would just let him take it where he wished; he was keen to tell his side of the story.

'They are so much . . . to blame, simply that! Mom has always been using drugs, prescribed, sure . . . but nonetheless, she's got that gene, the addiction gene . . . so do I . . . it's just so not fair . . . I can't help but wonder if my kids will be the same . . . and if so, if there is anything I can do about it . . . it may be too bloody late now . . . we're all screwed!' He was angry, confused, and feeling somewhat helpless.

Max went on to describe further how, in so many ways, it was the fault of his parents that he was as he was: addicted, unable to hold down a job, and now a father who had seemingly abandoned his own family. He described his father as a professionally successful but personally demanding man; if others, particularly Max, did not match up to his expectations and to his moral imperatives, then they were 'rejected . . . and discarded'. Because of this, Max never felt accepted or valued, particularly by his father, and this was the validation that he prized most.

64 Case vignette: The family

I wondered what made this approval from his father so important, and put the question to Max. I knew it might sound naive, but responses to such probes can be illuminating for both speaker and listener, even if they are critiqued as an obvious point.

'To have Dad, even a little, notice that I have, or that I do try, and that the failings aren't all my f***ing fault . . . that at least would relieve some pressure on me . . . yeah, actually, it would mean that I can fail, sometimes, but not be a total waste of space . . . I could try again, maybe try differently . . .'

There was a brief moment of eye contact at the conclusion of this comment, and Max seemed to relax ever so slightly.

Max then went on to describe his own relationship to his two sons. He expressed his pride in their school performances; he was the one who attended the parent–teacher consultations and the sports events when he was able. He told them often that he was proud of who they were as much as for what they had accomplished. He hoped that they did not suffer the same low self-opinion he had of himself, and he wondered if he would ever be able to offer them further support and guidance—but he recognised that this was on the condition that he was able to manage his own problems.

He felt that his parents could help him by granting him a safe haven for a time while he tried to get help for his addiction and attempted to reconnect with his wife and children.

It was apparent that Max desired reconciliation with his own family, and that he felt that he did have some potential, some possibility, to redirect his life, and to contribute to the well-being of others.

I asked if he thought a renewal, or a revision, of his relationship with his parents was also a possibility.

'I never could really make him proud of me; I just wasn't good enough, and never would be . . . hopeless, just . . . not going to happen.' Although this was stated with some frustration and anger, Max stifled a sob.

I recognised that this affirmation would go a long way to improving Max's self-concept, but I chose to set aside this possibility for the time being; I needed to hear what his parents' concerns were before any proposals were fielded.

It was only necessary to summarise Max's perspective at this point; I did so, focusing on the issue of responsibility as he saw it, including his desire to reconcile with his own family, and then asked if there was anything further. There was, so I set aside my plan to bring this session to a close, for now.

Case vignette: The family   65

'Yes . . . you need to know that I don't really like who I have become . . . I can see it, in the faces . . . of Dad, Mom . . . and my wife. They despise me, or pity me, or both . . . the kids were sometimes afraid of me, and I don't like what I see in the mirror, either . . . I don't recognise myself, and I don't know if I can get back to who I was, or to how I wanted to be.'

I allowed a long pause, but before I could break it, he added:

'I know I still need help. I want them to help me . . . it can only be them . . .'

'What makes it so important that it is them?'

'I can have the chance to show them that I can be a better person, that I can pull myself out of this mess and do it right this—is the place to start.'

I offered a brief reflection of his comment, then closed the session by reminding him of the confidentiality of our talk, and that I would come back to speak to him again in a short while.

Before I left him, I suggested he give further thought as to specifically how his parents might help him, and how he might help himself, considering his hopes to become a better parent and to reconnect with his family. I told him that we could explore this further, if he wished, in our next session.

I walked slowly down the hallway to the other room to meet with Mr. and Mrs. H. I took the time to think about what I had heard, and then with a deep breath, I put this aside in order to attend more fully to the people I was about to be with.

Mr. and Mrs. H had helped themselves to tea, and had obviously been talking; Mrs. H looked aggravated and restless, Mr. H a bit tearful but composed.

'What does he have to say for himself?' demanded Mrs. H.

Before I could remind her of the confidentiality of the sessions, Mr. H intervened: 'Martha, let's take our time for the moment. We can, and need to, tell our side of the story . . . in fact, I would like to know more about what you think . . . what we should, or can, do now . . . and maybe our facilitator has some suggestions too.'

I commented, as a reminder, that the possibilities for resolution were entirely under their own control, all of them, together; I was here purely as a facilitator in discovering and reviewing their options.

I asked them to share their views on the current dilemma.

They proceeded to tell me about many occasions in recent months when they, particularly Mr. H, had had to 'rescue' Max from some deplorable situation. There was an instance when the priest from their

66 Case vignette: The family

church had recognised Max as he staggered through the rain-filled gutters in the city centre, drunk, muddied, and bloodied, and the cleric had called them to pick Max up, literally, off the street.

There was another occasion when Max had tried to assist a young mother with her groceries as she struggled to manage her young child while packing the car, but Max was again intoxicated, and had so frightened the woman with his insistence on helping her that she called for help and the police arrived. Max was taken into custody, and his father had made apologies, and Max was let off with a severe warning.

In spite of many more such incidents, Mr. H remained steadfast in his assertion that Max could be helped, although he wasn't sure exactly how, and that they were the ones to provide that help, perhaps with some assistance from an addiction counsellor.

Mrs. H had a distinctly different view on this matter; she feared for her husband's well-being in the face of this enormous burden and trouble. Mr. H had spent many sleepless nights waiting for Max to come home from a night out, always vigilant in case he would be called upon to extricate his son from another unsavoury, if not dangerous, predicament; it had taken its toll on his health, and he suffered from exhaustion and prolonged anxiety.

'You have done, are doing, the best that you could, Jack; it is now also a terrible problem for me, as I feel that you too are at risk, and I couldn't bear it if . . . It's time we put it back to him, we cannot save him from himself . . . and perhaps we shouldn't, even if we could . . . ' Mrs. H stood up and paced behind the sofa, then sat down as she concluded.

'He has to learn to help himself. We are all responsible for ourselves, ultimately . . . can he, will he, come around to seeing this? But we cannot go on like this . . . I won't!'

'I almost . . . can't help it . . .' started Mr. H. 'Maybe I *am* a big part of the problem. I thought that I was helping him by not babying him, by not making it too easy for him . . . we both know life just isn't easy . . .' Mr. H looked toward me, and stated with some desperation, 'I thought I was doing the best thing for him, and now I still don't seem to know what that is . . .'

We sat in silence for a short while, and then Mr. H said, 'I'm sorry, Martha; I didn't realise how really difficult this has been for you . . . or how . . . I just felt that as he blames me for his problems, whether we agree or not, it appears that I am the one who has to fix it . . .'

Mr. H shifted in his seat to face me directly. 'There is something of a story behind this relationship between my son and me . . .'

He recounted how at Max's birth, the doctors had charged him with the most difficult decision of his life: because of complications with the

Case vignette: The family 67

delivery, Mr. H had to choose between saving his soon-to-be-born child and saving his wife. With very little time to deliberate, he had chosen his wife.

Although the result of the birth was nothing short of miraculous, as both mother and child were saved, Mr. H had always felt a deep sense of guilt about this incident. He declared that he "felt it in my bones' that Max somehow knew about this event, and the preference that he had demonstrated.

As a result, Mr. H had always felt that he had to compensate for what he saw as a failure to love his son enough. He hoped to demonstrate his affection and care by challenging Max to live up to the potential that he surely possessed, and that would make his father proud. If this strategy had succeeded, according to Mr. H, Max would have established a life that would be self-sufficient, satisfying, and productive.

It was a great shock, even now, to realise that these efforts had not, and were not, effective; it left Mr. H feeling even guiltier, and even more at a loss to decide what might be best for Max, and now, best also for his wife.

We discussed these revelations at some length, and the couple also recognised that Max's wife and children were also entangled in this dilemma. Without input from them, there was no way of knowing what might be needed or wanted by them. In the short term, it was considered that the better route to looking after them was to look after Max, and allow him to address those relationships.

Mr. H commented that on the rare occasions that they had to visit with Max and his family, they had been very pleased to witness Max in his roles as father and husband. He was loving and gentle; it was apparent that he had, in fact, the capacity to be reliable, caring, and responsible.

I summarised the perspective of Mr. and Mrs. H: they shared a deep concern for Max and for his relations with his family, which also had implications for them, as they were keen to participate in the lives of their grandchildren. Additionally, they felt—though more so on Mr. H's part—that it was possible to help Max in some way, but as things were currently, the situation was taking its toll on them both. Mr. H acknowledged the profound effect this was having on his wife, and also that a new strategy might be more effective in terms of assisting Max to regain a life that he wanted; additionally, this plan must also have less destructive consequences for the older couple.

As I intended to close the session and have another private meeting with Max, I asked Mr. and Mrs. H if there was something they wanted Max to know, something they felt it would be useful for him to

68 Case vignette: The family

understand. I suggested they consider this in my absence, and said that I would return for further discussions. However, this idea appealed to them, so they said they would like to take the opportunity to forward, via me, a message that they hoped would ease the tensions and that would support Max.

The message they wished me to pass on was that they wanted to help Max in some way, but that they weren't sure how at this moment, and that they had confidence that he could, and would, 'find himself' in a way that would allow him, his family, and his parents to re-establish happier, healthier relationships.

I commented that it seemed that not only was this a message for Max, but that it would be an important and desirable result for them too.

I reminded them that I could bring back a response only if I was given permission to do so, and also requested some discretion to present this message when I thought it was appropriate.

I thanked them for their candour, and excused myself.

When I met with Max again, he was visibly agitated.

I asked if he had further thoughts about what we had spoken about. He answered that he was again furious with both his parents: his mother was a hypocrite and had her own drug problem, and his father had had a long-term affair with his business accountant. So, according to Max, neither of them was in a position to criticise or give advice.

Max felt that his parents owed him another chance; everyone had 'screwed up' in some way, and not everyone always had to pay for their mistakes. And in truth, he had nowhere else to go, other than back to the streets.

Max commented: 'You know, I may not be educated, like you, or like my father, but hey, I have learned what I really need to know just from life . . . yeah, even from my so-called mistake . . . that's real learning . . . and I managed to take care of my family until I got caught up with the booze again . . .'

If this had been therapy, I would undoubtedly have addressed the comment made in reference to me; however, this process had slightly different aims, so I attended to those issues that were relevant in this context.

Max sat forward in his chair. 'I don't think they really know me, and never have! They never bothered! They just wanted me to be a regular member of society so that they didn't have to concern themselves with me anymore . . .'

'Okay, so you really do think you deserve, and can make something of, another chance . . . you can see yourself as a good 'family man', if you just get a break now . . . but you're not sure your parents really give a damn about you, or your hopes . . . is that how you see it?'

Case vignette: The family   69

Max relaxed back into his seat. 'Yeah, that is about it . . .'

I waited, reflecting on what had transpired.

I felt this might be the time to relay the message I had been given; Max seemed to have some trust in me, as I had been able to adequately reflect his view, and the nature of the communication might serve to address some of Max's concerns.

As it turned out, Max was very pleased, if somewhat surprised, to hear this statement; he was curious as to why it had never been verbalised, but he was noticeably impressed, and heartened, to hear that his parents did hold such a strong belief in him and his possibilities.

He responded with a message of gratitude for this vote of confidence, and a simple statement about his wish to have their help, and that winning, and maintaining, their confidence meant a great deal to him. He also indicated that he was prepared to listen to what arrangements they thought they would be willing to offer, and what kind of cooperation would be needed from him.

This seemingly modest message paved the way for further discussions. It became clear that, although everyone had something to lose, they also recognised that there were possibilities to realise some of their intentions and values.

Bit by bit, the process moved towards some agreed conditions. The messages passed backwards and forwards became more candid and emotional, and promoted clarity about hopes and intentions. There continued to be occasional outbursts of frustration, anger, and also goodwill and affection.

The mediation continued until late afternoon, at which point we met together to formalise an agreement.

The family members agreed that Max would continue to reside with his parents for another six months. During this time, he would spend the weekends in a residential rehabilitation centre to help him deal with his addiction problems as well as his relational difficulties. This allowed Mr. and Mrs. H to have their weekends to themselves, confident that Max was being well looked after.

Mr. and Mrs. H also agreed to provide an 'allowance' for Max on a weekly basis. This would provide him with funds to investigate employment opportunities and to have something of a social life.

Max agreed to a curfew, which would for the most part preclude any late-night activities. This eased the tensions for and between the parents, and also provided more opportunity for family meals and social activities that involved everyone.

It was discovered that Max's father-in-law, who was an attorney, had threatened to take out a restraining order on Max just prior to his

70   Case vignette: The family

departure from his family. It was decided that Mr. H would contact Max's in-laws to inform them of the current arrangement and of their collaborative plans for Max.

Meanwhile, Max would contact his wife, explain the current situation, ask for her forgiveness and patience, and request some limited contact with their children.

After these conditions had been written out, all present signed it and agreed that if there were further complications with respect to this contract, they would return for further facilitated mediation.

Reflections

It is so often the case, particularly in family disputes, that seemingly obvious communications have not been offered, or not been heard, or even been ignored. The content of these messages is often about mistaken assumptions, unspoken intentions, and much-needed information about aspirations and expectations.

I had some difficulty bracketing my own bias on the issue of responsibility. Max claimed that his addictive behaviour was the result of circumstances beyond his control; if this had been therapy, I might have explored this perspective further. I would not be interested in contesting his view; rather, I would have invited him to consider it for himself, to ascertain *how true* this premise was, how other beliefs aligned with or contradicted this premise, and what possibilities and limitations were produced by this stance.

As it was, in Max's world-view, he blamed his addiction problem on the genetic and behavioural legacy of his parents, yet he did feel he had scope to construct some kind of different and desirable future. He exercised his freedom to adopt an attitude towards that which he felt was inevitable: he might remain an addict, but could choose how to behave in spite of this fact; the future could be different than the past, and he wanted it to be.

It was important for Max to become, and be seen as, a good parent and a worthy son; these were two primary aspirations. He also felt he 'deserved' a second chance; there was something there he felt was worth the effort.

To feel that they were, and were also experienced as, credible parental figures was an ambition shared by Mr. And Mrs. H; there was common ground between the parties in terms of these values, which had not been previously appreciated by them.

These desires to be experienced in particular ways were accepted and acknowledged, first by me and then amongst the family members. In

Case vignette: The family 71

many ways, these expectations were also served in part by the conditions of the agreement.

Time was an issue for all concerned. The grandparents missed the occasions to be involved with their son and his family, and Max was anxious to become, as soon as possible, the kind of father he hoped to be. Everyone felt the pressure of time passing and of prolonged suffering.

All those involved were faced with uncertainty and change, and the relationship between these two issues. Change was acknowledged as a necessary condition for improvement in the situation, and in some ways it was difficult to choose what kind of change might be the most effective, for all involved. The contract became viewed as an 'experiment', which meant that further modifications could be made to accommodate the meanings and values that were being practically implemented.

Max and his parents experienced a great deal of anxiety in the face of what they saw as 'failures' and missed opportunities. The 'death' of certain possibilities, like changing the past, was recognised and acknowledged. As is so often the case, regrets functioned as motivation to avoid accruing more of the same as a result of sedimented perspectives and behaviour.

All those who were immediately affected by this predicament experienced and expressed their discomfort in bodily manifestations. Emotional experiences, such as anger and relief, were manifest in gestures and behaviours, and language was employed to dramatise those values that were implicated in the situation.

The world-views of the family members, with respect to this specific context, were disclosed from the very beginning.

Max believed that, cosmologically, he was a victim of circumstances that were 'unfair', and that this mitigated his responsibility for some of his behaviour; Mr. and Mrs. H were more inclined to subscribe to the view that a person could react to or engage with those aspects of life that are beyond one's control in a manner that might alleviate some suffering.

In reference to expectations regarding oneself, Max keenly felt he had let himself down, and although he saw this as somewhat understandable, considering the circumstances, he came to appreciate, similarly to his parents, that there was scope for improvement in his behaviour as well as his predicament. Max harboured hopes that he could change his attitude, as he already had evidence of this, and that this might help to improve matters.

Mr. and Ms. H felt that they had been somewhat off the mark in realising their hopes to be competent parents. They were in agreement that this was important to them both, but that they had, in spite of their good intentions, not satisfactorily realised this ambition. They were

72 Case vignette: The family

hopeful that this value might be better realised with the recent plans for living and working with their son to improve all their lives.

All those involved, to some extent, were initially invested in blaming others for their own regrets and disappointments: when Max didn't meet his parents' expectations, they became stern and critical; when Mr. and Mrs. H didn't perform as the parents Max expected them to be, he too became rejecting and hurtful.

Max expected the world at large to agree with his view that he was only marginally responsible for his behaviour due to extenuating circumstances. When this consensus was denied him, he became aggressive and belligerent, and continued to self-harm in the form of substance abuse, to prove his point and to 'punish' others as well as himself.

Mr. and Mrs. H were deeply embarrassed by their son's behaviour, and would have preferred that their difficulties remained private; they didn't believe that the world at large would tolerate, or forgive, their son for his actions, and felt that they too would be reproached for how they had raised Max as well as for how they handled this current situation.

The family members came to recognise that they did share a great deal of common ground: they wanted and valued many of the same things, but were conflicted about how to actualise them, and were all stuck with blaming and self-deprecation. Due primarily to recognition of these intentions and an appreciation that they could all assist each other in bringing about their aspirations, they moved from a combative and defeated position to one of collaboration.

Part II

The practice of facilitative conflict resolution

Conflict resolution is an endeavour that has been taking place ever since one individual wanted something from another, and the request was refused. In ancient times, this matter would have been referred to an elder, a religious leader, a shaman, or a wise woman for adjudication. In many instances, a verdict would have imposed orders on the challengers, in accordance with laws or cultural and social policies.

The imposition of a judgement prescribed by law and social norms has, and still maintains, a rather limited repertoire of possibilities for resolution; the values, aspirations, and desires of those directly involved are relegated in the service of popular decrees. Additionally, public exposure and possible humiliation are also consequences of the legal process; regardless of the righteousness of those involved, information that would have otherwise remained private can be damaging.

The principle of personal responsibility, the validity of subjective truth, and the recognition of ethical dilemmas are philosophical and sociological proposals that underpin an appreciation of the very personal and subjective nature of conflict and resolution. Such events were not just a matter of 'irrational' demands or perspectives, but were dilemmas sourced in private logic, and in the assumptions and values which constituted a person's world-view.

Such principles do not require extensive familiarity with legal matters or procedures; facilitative conflict resolution is as much an attitude as an acquired skill or format. This will be described in the following sections, and the strategies, practices, ethics, and process that are the extension of this attitude will be outlined.

Mediation is a form of alternative dispute resolution (ADR). It provides an alternative to arbitration, negotiation, adjudication, and, in the extreme scenario, aggression.

74 Part II: Facilitative conflict resolution

In its most basic form, it can be described thus:

> Mediation is a form of Alternative Dispute Resolution (ADR) whereby a 'third party neutral' intervenes to *facilitate* and assist the disputing parties in reaching a mutually acceptable settlement... The mediator will help by seeking to identify common aims and objectives, by re-opening lines of communication and by developing mutually acceptable proposals for settlement... the transition from a position of conflict to a position where they can form a 'working alliance'. (Strasser and Randolph 2004, p. 62)

The alliance referred to here is twofold: in the first instance, it is formed between the parties and the mediator, and in the second, it is formed between the parties.

The mediator working in a facilitative manner eschews imposing a solution, even if they are empowered to do so; they seek instead to ease the way, or to create the opportunity, for those embroiled in the conflict to discover their own agendas, which may not be fully understood in the heat of the defensive position.

By virtue of this aim, this form of mediation offers the possibility of settlement agreements that incorporate conditions *beyond the power or interests of the court*. Examples of this are apologies, expressions of sentiment, exchanges of personal views and intentions, collaborative and mutually beneficial activities, and practical arrangements (for example, the reorganisation of office space to accommodate better communication, or behavioural experiments in family contexts).

In this process, the mediator recognises and demonstrates the perspective that the parties are the experts on the dispute, and therefore on the resolution. Additionally, this stance supports a 'purer' stance of impartiality: if the dispute does not settle, it is not the problem of the mediator; they have no particular interest in compelling an agreement. This perspective is aligned with the concept that the facilitator, as well as those involved, can never be absolutely certain of the 'right' decision; it is the parties' responsibility to choose, and thereby 'own' the consequences.

Facilitative mediation is in direct contrast to what is commonly known as 'evaluative' mediation. Evaluative mediation is a mode of ADR in which the mediator, by virtue of some form of expertise, be it legal, commercial, or technological, for example, is invested by the parties with the remit to offer possible settlement scenarios based on the merits or weaknesses of the case. This proposal may or may not be

Part II: Facilitative conflict resolution 75

binding, according to the nature of the evaluation, and the prior agreement of the parties.

Evaluative mediation poses some difficulties. The mediator in this role has mitigated their impartiality; they may have an investment in acquiring a settlement to substantiate their expertise and fulfil the expectations of the clients, and, more significantly, the justification for the proposed settlement becomes 'objective' and impersonal.

And, perhaps more notably, evaluative mediation is likely to preclude the philosophical and therapeutic effects that facilitative mediation can offer.

Strasser and Randolph make these observations about evaluative style mediation:

> it discourages *self*-evaluation, prevents self-determination, promotes positioning, results in polarization and encourages parties to focus on their rights and liabilities rather than their interests and needs. (Strasser and Randolph 2004, p. 68)

The sections in Part II demonstrate the integration of the philosophical and psychotherapeutic tenets described in Part I. It will become apparent that there are few 'techniques' as such for the process of facilitation; it is rather a quality of relatedness and a mode of being-with that are advocated as conditions that may allow for an appreciation of choice, responsibility, and of the latitude to modify one's viewpoint on the current events and dilemma.

The sections describe attitude, process, practice, strategies, protocol, and ethics, all contexts for the naive enquiry that is a basis for dialogical engagement.

Cohn makes a statement with reference to psychotherapy that is equally relevant for the process and practice that will be described here as facilitative mediation:

> The practice is, so to speak, the other side of our beliefs. Practice is not the 'application' of ideas generated somewhere and passed on to somewhere else. Rather it is the enactment of our belief. (Cohn 2002, p. 116)

It is this author's belief that a mediator who understands the significance of the world-views held by the parties involved in dispute is more likely to achieve agreement that reflects the values and intentions of those in conflict; this allows for a greater understanding of and for those involved, and thus grants the opportunity for a therapeutic effect.

References

Cohn, H.W. 2002 *Heidegger and the Roots of Existential Psychotherapy*, Continuum, London.

Strasser, F. and Randolph, P. 2004 *Mediation: A psychological insight into conflict resolution*, Continuum, London.

Chapter 9

Attitudes about conflict and resolution

As with most of the significant events of life, it is useful to give some considered thought to one's attitude towards conflict; this is essential if one hopes to make constructive use of this eventuality either as a facilitator or as a party in a dispute.

We have seen that freedom, even in its contextualised and somewhat limited form, is a given of human existence. It follows that impediments to the exercise of anyone's freedom will be seen and experienced as a contest. One person or group has an intention, desire, or need that they wish to see served or actualised, and an opposing group or person refuses to grant the necessary cooperation in the realisation of these needs and ambitions.

The reasons for such opposition are numerous and various, but what one can be assured of is that each of the opposing parties views the intentions of their rivals as antithetical to their own values, expectations, hopes, and assumptions, that is, to their world-views.

Spinelli writes:

> existential psychotherapy's approach to conflict is not primarily about its alteration, reduction, or removal. Instead it suggests that the therapist's task is to assist the client in focusing upon, and connecting more adequately the perceived source of conflict with, the worldview that shapes and defines it. (Spinelli 2007, p. 66)

This is certainly a sage attitude when considering one's approach to or involvement in conflict.

Even at the level of kingdoms and countries, the world-views of those involved are evident. Those who lead wish to be seen as the source of power and protection for their constituents; those governors or heads of state will employ whatever strategies are necessary to maintain the power (or the illusion of power) invested in them by their followers or

78 Attitude

subordinates. Such strategies, like the conquest of other tribes or countries, also serve to indicate that these leaders are graced by the blessing of higher powers; their victories are offered as proof that the deities support their cause (I refer the interested reader to Ernest Becker's anthropological treatise on the nature of violence, *Escape from Evil*, 1975). All of these manoeuvrings serve the function of maintaining and actualising the world-views of individuals, societies, and cultures.

These disputes can refer to the distribution of resources, to the acquisition of power and control, or to the aspiration to be experienced in some way by others. It is this latter intention that is most often the source of everyday difficulties in most contemporary societies.

I often request of those in attendance at seminars to share a recent conflict situation, and I may suggest that such an occurrence could be fleeting and modest. Perhaps this morning someone had angry words with someone else who jumped the queue at the taxi ramp, or with a caller from a utility company erroneously claiming that their account was in arrears. These may seem like low-level challenges, but the dynamics at play are very similar to those involved in a more perilous or highly charged dispute that may involve military and political actions. The vignettes offered by those in attendance quite readily illustrate the principles outlined here, and it becomes evident that these proposals are generally applicable to all disputes.

What is apparent is that conflict at various levels is in fact pretty much an everyday occurrence. How we engage with this dynamic will reflect our own world-views, and will impact on the quality of our own lives and those of others; in this sense, our behaviour, which is informed by our attitude, is an ethical concern.

Early on in seminars in which I lecture on conflict and resolution, I ask those present: what is your first reaction to the word 'conflict'?

This question is purposefully vague. I leave it to those in the group to work through the replies until they come to the realisation, as they inevitably do, that their responses to an actual dispute are relative to the context, but how and why is often the subject of further discussion.

I can offer a scenario that illustrates this point. If I am standing at a bus stop and someone makes a critical remark on my clothing, I am likely to brush it aside with disdain. If, on the other hand, my husband suggests I should reconsider my choice of wardrobe for a particular event, then I am more likely to receive this challenging comment with at least irritation, if not a more indignant reaction. The distinction between the vignettes is probably obvious: I have a greater investment in how I am perceived by my partner than I am by a stranger whose opinion

Attitude 79

bears little threat to my self-concept; it would matter a great deal if I was rejected by my husband, but not so much by an unknown individual.

This is an example of how the *level of threat* to my values and assumptions about myself, and of others, is relative to the force of my reaction to the possible impediment to my aspirations.

Initial responses to the query put to the group generally indicate a negative attitude towards conflict: 'anger', 'aggression', 'powerlessness', 'defence', 'fear', 'emotional', and 'loss of control' are amongst the usual characterisations. Such reactions demonstrate intentions and hopes of avoiding this kind of encounter; it is viewed as an occasion that holds little hope of a productive outcome.

We all have an understandable fear of conflict. It is an emotionally charged encounter that often feels destabilising, especially as we do not know how we, or the other person, might react. These are the fundamental dual concerns: how far will I go in the face of this contest, and how extreme will the other person's reaction become?

And, as has been discussed earlier, uncertainty is anathema to most of us in most situations; it is a reminder that not only is *this* situation fraught with chaos, but that indeed, much of our existence is permeated with this quality.

Consequently, many people attempt to avoid any kind of conflict. This avoidance comes at some cost. In order to divert or deny the anxiety that attends a contest, we must retreat, or opt for a detour, and abandon our ambition to be heard and understood, as well as our opportunity to engage with the world and others in a manner that could be mutually beneficial. In such disengagement, we miss the opportunity to understand the people and obstacles that stand in our way. If and when such an opportunity is recognised and worked with, there is a greater possibility for cooperation in the actualisation, as well as the comprehension, of another's world-view and the projects it entails.

This attempt to avoid conflict is a common condition in marital dilemmas. It is dismaying to hear a couple claim, usually with some pride, that they rarely have arguments; however, they are now at a juncture that is untenable. This situation indicates that there are likely to be a great deal of uncommunicated hopes, assumptions, and expectations that have not been heard or served. These are not communicated, and are not properly 'heard', in part because the partners harbour fears that if they *truly hear* the other's concerns, their new understanding might necessitate a reconsideration, or modification, of their own perspective.

What they are resisting is the possibility of realising that they might be mistaken, even to some degree, which would demand a change in

80 Attitude

their world-view, and as has been noted, even a small alteration in any facet of the world-view will have implications for all aspects. Such a possibility of change is also correlated with uncertainty, as any alteration to our outlook or actions will have unknowable consequences.

Additionally, discovering that one is mistaken also implies responsibility for a plethora of consequences; one discovers that even with the best intentions, one can be characterised as 'guilty'.

It must also be recognised that when people *are* able to reach some understanding of each other's aspirations and intentions, this leaves them exposed to possible exploitation. Understanding brings with it the revelation of one's vulnerabilities.

This brings us to the issue of trust. Mistrust is a significant impediment to dispute resolution and reconciliation. To the extent that an Other cannot be trusted with the knowledge of one's vulnerabilities, there will be little room for collaboration.

The establishment, loss, and recovery of trust will be discussed further in subsequent sections, as it is an issue that can only be mitigated and mediated in a dialogical encounter in which all parties are willing to take some risks in order to serve some aspects of their world-view.

So, again, it would seem that not a day passes without contests or disputes of some kind, some of which are denied or avoided, some of which are ignored, some of which are occasions for forceful or manipulative strategies to implement one's own intentions, and some of which are encountered as an opportunity to come to a deeper understanding of self and others, and the fruitful cooperation that this might engender.

Sartre is quite clear that conflict is an inevitable event, a consequence of freedom, choice, and relatedness. He proposes:

> Conflict is the original meaning of 'being-for-others'. (Sartre 1993, p. 364)

This clearly indicates that for Sartre, conflict is an unavoidable occurrence in human existence; it isn't necessarily sought out as an option. In fact, one needs only to exist—to turn up, so to speak—to become embroiled in a challenge to one's 'projects', or to be seen as an obstruction to another person's intentions.

Then what can be hoped for in recognising this inevitability?

Spinelli comments on the aim of an existentially informed perspective on conflict, particularly with reference to the element of collaboration:

reciprocity involves both conflicting parties' simultaneous attempts to make themselves the vehicle for the other's project rather than seek to make the other the object of his or her own ends. (Spinelli 2007, p. 67)

As suggested earlier, the cycle of contest and collaboration is continuous. In understanding conflict, either as one directly involved or acting as a mediator, it is vital to appreciate this ubiquitous dynamic. It is hoped that one may come to recognise that, as with any eventuality, it holds positive possibilities as well as perils.

In fact, from an existential perspective, the denial or avoidance of the inevitable is often the source of much psychological distress.

Cohn comments:

The existential therapist proposes that it is unaccepted aspects of existence itself which are at the core of the disturbance. (Cohn 1997, p. 24)

This assertion indicates in what way a conflict situation can be a therapeutic opportunity: to accept that it is an eventuality, and to choose to engage with it directly. This is the kind of change that existential psychotherapy promotes; we respond to the 'givens' of existence, we can *choose to choose*, and in so doing, we become the authors of our lives instead of the (putative) victims of circumstance.

This stance is often referred to as 'authenticity' or 'good faith'. And there are further advantages to an authentic position:

The possible benefit of an authentic engagement with life is the realisation of our power to value things as one sees fit, even if these evaluations are subject to impermanence. An authentic attitude frees us to choose freely. (Iacovou and Weixel-Dixon 2015, p. 51)

When conflict is understood as an inevitable aspect of relatedness, and to the extent that there is a hopeful and genuine dialogue between challengers, there is a possibility for cooperation in the exercise of agency; not all will be lost, and one can come to recognise what one is willing to compromise or even sacrifice for the values that are given priority in a given context.

The next time around, different values and intentions will be gained and lost, and we may come to recognise that by engaging with the inevitable, we actually maintain some power in realising our world-view, and in assisting others in doing the same.

References

Cohn, H. 1997 *Existential Thought and Therapeutic Practice*, Sage, London.
Iacovou, S. and Weixel-Dixon, K. 2015 *Existential Therapy*, Routledge, London.
Sartre, J.P. (1943) 1993 *Being and Nothingness* (trans. H.E. Banes), Routledge, London.
Spinelli, E. 2007 *Practising Existential Psychotherapy: The relational world*, Sage, London.

Chapter 10

A theory of emotions and how to work with them

Emotions are one of the most misunderstood aspects of human existence. They are often viewed as the opposing force to reason, and an obstacle to a 'realistic' perspective.

In the existential perspective, emotions are recognised as a valuable source of information. They tell us something about how we find ourselves in the situation, in the world.

Heidegger (1993) proposes that we are always 'attuned' in some way with respect to our context. Polt comments:

> I am always attuned in some way to my *overall* situation. This is how I am there—or, better, how I am my 'there' . . . moods are *disclosive* . . . For example, fear does not cut us off from things—to the contrary, it reveals something as a threat. (Polt 1999, p. 66)

Heidegger states that moods give us a more essential understanding than do factual statements (1993); one may have a great deal of factual information about an event or a situation but fail to appreciate the overall mood or emotional timbre. Our emotional experience is one way we both understand and *participate* in the situation.

So if we dismiss or deny or distort a mood or emotion, we deprive ourselves of some useful information about *how we are* in our current context. This is often the case when we have an emotional experience that is uncomfortable, or one that we consider 'inappropriate'. Feelings that bear this latter characterisation are those that do not 'suit' who we think we are, or how we would like to be. They are at odds with our self-concept, and so are relegated.

Similarly, if we ignore or deny the emotional content of others' communications, we may lose the opportunity to appreciate the values and assumptions that are relevant to the current relationship and context.

84 A theory of emotions

This is not to say that reason should be subordinated, but rather that both or all functions should be valued equally. Cognition, reason, embodiment, and emotion are aspects of 'a living whole' (Macquarrie 1973, p. 156).

The proposals so far on this topic have further implications, particularly as they reflect the propositions previously considered in the sections on phenomenology and hermeneutics.

What may be apparent is that emotions are not just forces 'inside' our heads. They are one way we are connected to the world, and they are *about* being-in-the-world; in the language of phenomenology, emotions are *intentional*.

There is a 'what' and a 'how' in the invariable dynamic of perception known as 'intentionality', as was clarified previously; this is easily illustrated in the case of emotions as well. All emotional experience is *about* something: if I am happy, I am happy *about* something; if I am angry, I am angry *about* something. But what this something *is*, is often not explored or reflected upon.

In a typical illustration, it is quite common for families who come together to discuss their problems to confess that they are unclear about what exactly is causing the distress. There may be ostensible particularities that are dismaying or irritating, but these often do not seem to 'add up' in a way that would justify the more extreme anger or rage that is being experienced and expressed (and this qualification is put forward by those directly involved).

Upon reflecting on these feelings, there are a few notable factors that typically come to light. There are a number of emotions involved, for every party, and these are directly correlated to aspects of the world-view, and the values and assumptions which it comprises. The understanding of what is at stake unfolds, and new perspectives and possibilities come into view.

An example of such a predicament is parents who may be at odds over how to educate their children. What makes this important may be how this choice reflects on them as parents, or as members of the community, or with reference to the ambitions they hold for their offspring. If the nature of these aspirations is not shared, at least to some extent, then the lack of collaboration necessary between the adults to actualise any intentions will be impeded, resulting in a dispute.

What is very apparent is that the question needs to be raised: what makes this or that choice *so* important that it is worth a serious conflict, in which other values, like harmony or respect, are compromised? Such an exploration helps to clarify what one is willing to give up in order to actualise some other aspiration.

A theory of emotions   85

What emerges from a focused and timely exploration of the various feelings involved is that there are a number of possible losses in terms of values and expectations. These liabilities themselves are sometimes, in fact often, in competition with each other.

As in the example above, one parent may be conflicted about sending their children to a private school, as this does not represent their political views; on the other hand, the same parent may recognise that that option may provide better opportunities for the child. If neither of these concerns is shared by the other parent, then there is little hope of having either of the values realised, and the loss is magnified.

Additionally, until they are faced with this choice, the parental couple may have assumed that they shared at least similar perspectives on the issue; when the time comes to choose and act, priorities may be altered. At such a juncture, the couple may feel challenged, and disappointed and angry, that the partner has changed their view, or that they *haven't* changed their view on the decision in light of considered reflection. Again, this may leave one or both of the partners anxious, uncertain, and threatened: who *is* this person with whom I thought I shared my values, and what does it mean about *who I am, and who we are*?

The effect of such a conflict can have far-reaching consequences for those involved. It is understandable that it is a highly charged emotional experience, considering what might be compromised or lost.

Another notable characteristic of the emotional experience is that it is dynamic. Emotions are fluid, changeable; it is difficult to hold on to any one emotion. It is for this reason more appropriate to refer to a person who is angry, sad, etc., rather than to designate someone as an 'angry person', a 'sad person', and so on. A single emotional event cannot totalise anyone, as these are constantly changing and represent only a part of what it is to be a person.

And, as described in the vignette above, more than one emotion is present at any given time. When carefully considered, emotional experience is multi-layered, complex. This is commonly expressed in statements like 'I am angry with her, but I am also sad that it has come to this'. If one was to query further about the anger and the sadness, it is likely that the core issue would be loss of some sort, either pending or past.

It is frequently the case, in a dispute, that the loss of a future that was worked for and hoped for is one of the most difficult events to process. The loss of a child is such an event, as is the notification of a debilitating or terminal health condition.

As has been discussed, the world-view is the collection of our assumptions, expectations, and aspirations and values about ourselves,

86 A theory of emotions

others, the world, and the cosmos. The realisation of these elements is what constitutes purpose in life. We are looking to the future to maintain what has been realised, as well as considering what choices and strategies we need to adopt to implement those aspects that have not been sufficiently served.

When our world-view is actualised, and to the extent that it is actualised, we will experience emotions like happiness, contentment, and joy; when the actualisation is prevented, we will feel angry, fearful, anxious, and sad. On the occasions when another assists one in realising one's aspirations, there will be affinity, even love. In those instances where an other or others contest one's intentions, there will be strife, conflict, and defence.

It is for this reason that emotions can be recognised as *the voice(s) of values*. We are emotional about values; we are invested in their implementation and acknowledgement. We are purposeful entities who strive to affect and mould our world according to our intentions.

It is our ambition to actualise our values that informs our choices of behaviour. *Emotions are not the drive behind behaviour.* Rather, we are stretching out towards the future, to purposefully implement our values, aspirations, expectations, and desires.

In a conflict situation, it is the emotions that indicate which values and aspects of the world-view are implicated in this situation. The emotional expressions and content should be appreciated for the insights they can provide.

And, as the emotions are explored for the references they hold about the world-view, the perspective of the person whose private logic is represented in their world-view *can change*. As the values that are impeded gain clarity, the person is better placed to consider what options will best serve their hopes, and which compromises may be necessary to make these come to fruition.

An example of this process might be illustrated with the exploration of a commonly heard statement in disputes: "I am angry they haven't apologised by now!" When the speaker is questioned as to what it is exactly about this that so angers them, they reply: "They seem to have no idea about how much this situation has hurt me and humiliated me!" It then comes to light that this apology, and the accompanying desire to continue the relationship, are actually more meaningful than the vindication of a court hearing or the vast amount of money that is being demanded.

This is what is meant by *movement* in a dispute situation. By virtue of exploration, reflection, and enquiry, the *horizon* of the person involved

A theory of emotions   87

changes; a different horizon allows a different view on the situation, and on possibilities as well as pitfalls.

If the information that emotions can produce with reference to the world-view are not explored, it is quite likely that those involved will remain stuck in and with the positions they arrived with; *they have no reason to move.* It is only when they discover their true purposes, that is, their ambitions for the future, and are able to acknowledge their losses as well as the possible gains, that any progress can be made towards an agreement.

It is this factor that is the therapeutic effect: one holds a deeper understanding of one's world-view and how it informs choices, and one discovers where one's agency, as well as one's vulnerabilities, lies.

It is also even more apparent that if disputes could be solved by virtue of reason alone, it would happen more frequently. Conflict always involves emotions, and these are the clues as to what the dispute is really about.

Finally, it is important to review concerns that are often articulated with respect to working with emotions.

Many people harbour anxieties about emotions, their own as well as those of other people. There is fear that emotion will 'overwhelm' them or the person they are with and that all reason, or negotiation, will come to a halt. More often than not, this is with respect to difficult emotions like grief or despair. Such an attitude harkens back to theories that assigned a compartmentalised structure to a human being. When viewed as a 'living whole', as existentialism claims, human beings are complex entities that include, at all times, feelings, cognitions, embodiment, assumptions, and aspirations. Any one of these aspects may be foregrounded, in expression and/or experience, but as these are all dynamic forces, there is constant movement and change.

One only needs to wait for things to change.

There is also a frequently expressed concern that allowing a person to 'wallow' in their emotional experience will somehow entrench them in their powerlessness or victimhood. This too is a misunderstanding of a complex entity. Humans are not totalised by a single emotion, experience, or communication: we are, as described in previous philosophical discussions, in the process of becoming.

It should also be noted that power and vulnerability are not mutually exclusive states. One can have control or power over some aspects and, at the same time, feel exposed or vulnerable in another regard.

It can be difficult to 'be' with someone as they express their difficulties; we all know what it is to suffer. But as a facilitator, or as one

88 A theory of emotions

involved in a contentious or problematic situation, it is vital that these emotional expressions be respected and appreciated; they should not be repressed, suppressed, or coerced (except in the most extreme cases of aggressive behaviour). It is often our own anxieties about our own powerlessness in the face of suffering that prompt us to attempt to close down a significant and useful expression. It is likely to be more helpful to abide with the person, knowing that this too will pass.

And if one is affected by the display of emotion of another person, one need only wait, for both joy and grief are episodic, and things will change. One should be more concerned if one lacks the capacity to be affected, as it is what connects us to the world and others.

References

Heidegger, M (1962) 1993 *Being and Time* (trans. J. Macquarrie and E. Robinson), Blackwell, Oxford.

Macquarrie, J. (1972) 1973 *Existentialism*, Penguin Books, London.

Polt, R. 1999 *Heidegger: An introduction*, UCL Press, London.

Chapter 11

Practice and skills in managing conflict and resolution

This discussion will provide examples of skills that can promote exploration of one's world-view, and also that of another's if one is acting as a facilitator.

However, it must be noted that these skills must be an extension of an attitude: this attitude is grounded in acceptance.

This kind of acceptance is about receiving and acknowledging the person(s) involved, including oneself, in exactly the place in which they *are* currently. 'Meeting', 'accepting', and 'receiving' are conditions that set the stage for explorations that can facilitate deeper understanding of oneself and of the elements that constitute one's world-view or that of another.

Spinelli describes this quality of acceptance with respect to psychotherapy, and designates it as an aspiration:

> the therapist's willingness and ability to 'stay with' what is present and is being presented, rather than 'moving on' to alternative ways of being that may appear to be preferable. (Spinelli 2007, pp. 60–61)

Such an attitude and willingness, that serves as the foundation for skills, exploration, and dialogue, can most effectively promote a trusting and open relationship.

If the facilitator cannot or will not adopt such an approach, albeit as an aspiration, the skills are likely to be experienced as attempts at manipulation. The facilitator, or the investigator, will be seen as the self-appointed expert on the choices and changes that the person should adopt. This can lead to defensiveness on the part of the person whose world-view is being characterised as flawed or inappropriate.

Such an accepting premise allows the person whose perspective is being considered to recognise and reflect on their position as it is, with its inherent liabilities, limitations, and possibilities. Such clarification can be the starting point for deciding how to change and whether to change.

It may be apparent at this juncture that the communication skills that will be outlined here are rooted in an attitude of 'being-with'. This is the context that informs both how, and what kind of, 'doing' will take place.

The being-with approach promotes collaboration in a dialogue. Such dialogue, as described previously in this text, allows for an unfolding of meaning and understanding; there is no need to direct the discourse, as the concerns and intentions that are most relevant will be revealed as they are encountered and discovered.

This can provoke a certain amount of anxiety for a facilitator. It can feel as if there is 'not much' happening. This concern is often related to one's need to be seen as competent or 'professional'.

This would be an example of an occasion when one's own agenda interferes with the process, and to the extent that it is not bracketed, it can result in derailing the enquiry.

This brings us to a review of the phenomenological method, as it is relevant to the kind of exploration we are hoping to effect.

The first rule of this 'method' is to bracket one's own assumptions and biases about the party or the situation (or oneself!). As suggested earlier, this is never completely accomplished; what is hoped for is that we can be aware, to some extent, of how our own world-view is aligned or diverges from that of the person we are with, in an effort to avoid imposing our own intentions. To the degree that this is accomplished, there will be a more expansive 'space' for the other person's perspective to come to light.

In facilitating or understanding a conflict situation, this would include one's own views on the situation or a possible agreement, as well as the desire to be the instigator of the same.

The second rule is to encourage description in the place of explanation or conclusions. This too includes the mediator, as it is hoped that the narrative remains at a descriptive level as long as is feasible.

For example, a party who is embroiled in a boundary dispute with a neighbour might seem to have a feeble case in terms of his legal rights, according to the facilitator. This evaluation may be noted and set aside in an effort to understand what aspects, other than the legal ones, are of importance to the narrator. There may come a time, once the party has had their concerns heard, acknowledged, and to some extent understood, that the mediator or the party may include the legal status of the claim as a consideration.

In the case of such a situation, the party would be asked to describe his experience in some detail—for example, what was it like to discover the fences had been moved? And in response to describing his family's outrage, how did the narrator feel about the reactions he witnessed from his family? What is he experiencing now as he tells the story?

It is usually at this stage of the exploration that a great deal of emotional experience will be communicated.

If the listener adopts a naive attitude, bearing in mind that it is best to bracket one's own assumptions, it can be highly effective to enquire about these expressions. If the speaker states that he is 'outraged' by the event, the query might be, 'What is it exactly about this that so enrages you?' If the narrator states, 'I am sorry it has come to this', the probe might be, 'What is it that you find sad about this predicament?'

The responses are likely to deepen the appreciation, for both listener and speaker, of the values that are involved in the situation being considered. It is unusual, if not rare, that one is invited to further consider the significance of their emotional experience; this is in line with the 'staying-with' approach of the dialogue. It also demonstrates a deep respect for all that the speaker is relaying.

Additionally, such an enquiry is likely to have the effect of revealing further emotional experiences, which, when followed through in the same manner, can provide further insight into the world-view that is impacted by the dilemma.

These insights, this information, alter the understanding of the situation under review. Such modifications can produce novel possibilities and choices.

The account being sought is a subjective one. It is not necessary to request an account of the facts; they will appear as the person describes their *experience of the facts*. And it is this that is of interest to a facilitative mediator. It is in this description, in which the facts are subjectively evaluated, that the values that are being contested will become clarified.

The facilitator too will be paraphrasing and summarising these descriptions, inviting correction or refinement from the other person, thereby offering their partial understanding of the other's viewpoint, until the speaker is exhausted, or satisfied that their position is sufficiently understood for the time being.

In support of this intention of 'staying-with', the listener should also hear the report without applying any hierarchy of importance to the particulars of the story; this is the third rule of the method.

It is tempting to focus on some aspect of the early report that would seem to indicate a possible measure of concession. Again, it is best to

92 Practice and skills

suspend this interest until the initial exploration seems to wind down, although not completely. All aspects of the narrative warrant equal attention until the speaker chooses to begin to prioritise their concerns.

The phenomenological attitude provides a framework for what might be called 'tuning in' (Strasser and Randolph 2002). This is the attempt to understand the world-view as it is implicated in the current situation, and it is best achieved by 'staying-with' the story as it is presented.

When this is adequately accomplished, the narrator will often return their attention to the dilemma at hand. This is indicated in comments like, 'I've told you my story; now what?'

At this juncture, the mediator may then 'tune out' along with the party, and may verify, via observations or questions, what concerns or aspects of the situation were emphasised or minimised in order to check on their own understanding. These observations may be summarised with respect *to what is important to the party*, as they have expressed it, and may include the facts as they have been experienced by the narrator.

Tuning in and tuning out are forms of listening. The former is an attempt to be 'alongside' the party, in an effort to share their horizon, that is, their perspective, even if this can only be achieved in some small part; the latter form of listening is when the facilitator accompanies the speaker as they return to the problem or situation at hand.

Tuning and tuning out are cyclical forms of listening and being-with; they remain as possibilities throughout any dialogue.

The skills referred to so far have been those that are usually found in anyone's repertoire of communication skills: paraphrasing, summarising, questioning, reflecting back, and observations. It should be noted that the questions posed concern how something is experienced, rather than clarification of the facts, and they are likely to be sourced in a naive attitude, resulting in 'open' questions that begin with 'how' or 'what', thereby suggesting that the facilitator is not expecting any particular response.

Interpretation is another verbal intervention that can be effective. However, we must recall the principles of hermeneutics to qualify this skill.

Cohn reports:

> hermeneutic interpretation does not replace what is already known with what is concealed, but any disclosure extends what is already known, and thus the understanding of the total situation . . . (Cohn 2002, p. 48)

Practice and skills   93

And every new understanding can generate novel choices and options, in much the same fashion as the unfolding in a dialogical engagement, and the creative spontaneity of discourse, as discussed previously.

This is still a manner of 'staying-with'; the interpretation is one that reflects the party's perspective and understanding. An example of this might be that the client discovers that they hold opposing goals. The facilitator might reflect this in saying, 'So, on the one hand, you want to be fair, but on the other, you feel you must retain some control in this situation'. Note that the facilitator does not add anything that has not been communicated already. To do so would be to impose their own interpretation, and may result in obstructing the party's own, personal clarification; it could also designate the listener as the 'expert' on a situation that belongs to the speaker.

There is also a very powerful and effective non-verbal intervention: silence.

Silence is not about doing nothing; it can be an elegant combination of being and doing.

Macquarrie quotes Karl Jaspers (1883–1969), a German philosopher and contemporary of Heidegger:

> We reach this silence not by refraining from thoughts or speech, but by carrying them to the extremes where they revert to silence. In time, they will shortly make us speak again. (Macquarrie 1973, p. 144)

Such silence, even as a short pause in the discourse, marks the occasion in which we pause to reflect on what has been said and what has been heard. It is in these breaks from the flow of speech that *we can hear ourselves* in what we have communicated. This is a necessary part of the dialogue. This is what can make the process therapeutic. We may reach a point where we feel understood, but then we realise that things have changed. The understanding that is the product of dialogue is not finished, is not complete, and is not total; a novel and more complicated meaning emerges, inclusive of previous perspectives, but modified by the concrete realisations that discourse provokes.

This movement is often evidenced in statements like 'Now that I have said that, . . .' or 'There is more to it than what I've just said, although that is what I believed'.

Things have changed; horizons are different. And this can be due in large part to an engagement in which the agendas of the listener are set aside in favour of an open, undetermined, dialogue.

94 Practice and skills

When a problem is understood in a different light, options are multiplied and liabilities can be traded off.

These few skills support a practise of dialogical engagement, in which those involved extend themselves instead of only defending themselves. These means of 'doing and being' will support the strategies to be described in the following section.

References

Cohn, H.W. 2002 *Heidegger and the Roots of Existential Therapy*, Continuum, London.

Macquarrie, J. (1972) 1973 *Existentialism*, Penguin Books, London.

Spinelli, E. 2007 *Practising Existential Psychotherapy: The relational world*, Sage, London.

Strasser, F. and Randolph, P. 2004 *Mediation: A psychological insight into conflict resolution*, Continuum, London.

Chapter 12

Strategies for facilitative conflict management

In the approach outlined in this text for an existential psychotherapeutic model for conflict management and solution, strategy does not refer to 'techniques' applied to coerce or manipulate people into agreement. To a very large extent, the strategies described here are those that provide the circumstances that are most likely to foster reflection on one's world-view, and how this is relevant to the current dilemma.

The most fundamental of these conditions is a trusting relationship with the people involved. This is true both for the parties in a dispute and for the facilitator for a conflict.

Trust is not an absolute; it is dynamic; it is tidal. It can be nurtured, won, lost, and regained. It is rarely total, and it is not necessarily permanent. Trust can be engendered almost immediately, or it can take some time and effort to generate.

There must be some level of trust between or amongst people if there is to be any collaboration whatsoever; it need be just enough to accommodate the situation at hand. In a dispute, there needs to be at least enough trust to reveal one's wants and intentions. Such disclosure can leave one exposed to possible exploitation or manipulation; it is therefore paramount that at least a modicum of trust is generated.

Trust is created when one's aspirations and values are heard and accepted. This can be accomplished with the kind of approach and skills described in the previous section; in fact, the purpose of adopting these is in the hope of fostering rapport and trust. When one's world-view is explored and appreciated with the assistance of another, or in the presence of another, one need not defend one's perspective quite so vehemently.

When someone is successful in adequately articulating, without judgement, the views of another, the person who is disclosing may then feel safe enough to consider their position. Hearing one's outlook articulated with some accuracy allows for the possibility, and the opportunity, to consider the vulnerabilities and assumptions that underpin their defence.

96 Strategies

This movement may be reflected in comments like 'Well, yes, there is some truth in what I've told you, but . . .' or 'You've understood what I intended, and you must also know . . ."

It is important that a mediator be attentive to these kinds of expressions; they indicate the possibility of a shift in perspective and intentions. At such a juncture, it is also wise to express some appreciation, in as genuine a manner as possible, for the candour in the disclosure; it demonstrates that due to some, even miniscule, level of trust (and perhaps need), the speaker is reconsidering their priorities.

Building trust, even at a very minimal level, rests on the acknowledgement, if not the actualisation, of a person's world-view. The aspect of this that is most readily addressed is that of relatedness. As proposed previously, we need others to confirm us in the ways in which we wish to be experienced. If I hope to be seen as kind, for example, there must be an Other that receives my kind acts and appreciates them as such.

In a dispute, it is essential to hear how the party, be it an individual or a group, wishes to be experienced. People may claim, 'You can see I am/ we are trying to be reasonable!' or 'I am doing the best I can to be a good parent'. It is essential to recognise these aspirations. To the extent that they can be acknowledged, trust will be generated and renewed when necessary. In a response that attends to this intent, a facilitator might comment, 'Yes, I can see that it is important for you to be recognised as a caring parent in this situation; how can we make that happen?'

This is an example of tuning in and out, a dynamic that may well take place in the course of a few seconds. It also helps the person to clarify further where their priorities lie—in 'winning', which holds the threat of significant losses, or (in this example) in fulfilling the more complicated ambition of being a worthy parent, by their own standards as well as those of others who are significant.

An additional issue that supports and affects strategy is one that is not actually created, but need only be acknowledged and noted to be effective: time.

As discussed previously, time is a 'given' of existence that impacts all aspects of life. It heralds death, change, limitations, and all facets of temporality, i.e., past, present, and future.

People in distress review the past very often in an effort to understand the cause of their predicament; it is hoped that the same mistake will not be repeated. However, this indicates an expectation that future circumstances will be exactly like those that were in place previously. This is not possible, as change is also inevitable, and circumstances, while they may appear similar, are not ever precisely the same.

Additionally, in reviewing past events, the speaker may find that the story is slightly different than the one they expected to report, especially in the presence of a listener. Already, there is a modification in how events are viewed and valued.

But most significantly, the narration is an effort to have the point of view understood and, hopefully, *agreed with*.

This is a distinction that raises concerns for those who hope to effect a shift in perspective; it is feared that understanding will be read as *agreement*.

To pre-empt this possibility, it is useful to preface a summary or paraphrase of the speaker's report with a statement like 'So from your perspective, it seems like . . .' or 'I can hear that from your point of view, . . .' This will make it clear that the speaker's outlook is understood, and accepted as *true for them now*.

This attitude is reminiscent of that regarding 'truth' in the expositions on phenomenology and hermeneutics: the truth is partial, mutable, and unfolds upon reflection. It is at these points that it may be recognised that the truth is complex and deeply personal.

It is frequently the case that when the person feels sufficiently understood by the listener, they themselves 'tune out' in the manner described previously, and they look to the future: how can this situation be remedied? The dilemma is currently uncomfortable, if not untenable, and the possibility of a resolution in which all is not lost may seem distant.

This is an important occasion in the process. There is an understanding that time is passing, and that it may be preferable to mitigate the suffering by reconsidering what values might be relegated in the hopes of concluding the dispute.

It is a difficult juncture for all involved. It is not easy to be with someone who is suffering and know that it is not advisable to attempt, or perhaps even possible, to assuage the distress.

The facilitator should respect this realisation, and may even reflect on the concern for time lost with the party. It can be useful to articulate this as a benefit in bringing this difficult episode to a close sooner rather than later.

However, it is worthwhile to linger with these realisations. To push towards an agreement would probably disadvantage the party; it is more appropriate to allow the time and space for them to think though this new position and consider how to proceed. The pressure of time has become apparent. Time may be better spent championing projects and aspirations that can more readily be realised; some compromise at this point may seem like a more palatable option.

98 Strategies

Additionally, one should not be too hasty in over-emphasising the advantages possible in making early concessions; there is always another side to the choice. If the mediator is remiss in exploring this, the trust engendered may be lost; it may appear that the mediator's agenda for reaching an agreement has taken priority over the client's intentions.

One should bear in mind that, when we say 'yes' to one option or ambition, we say 'no' to others. This principle was reviewed with respect to finitude and limitations; we can't have it all. We are finite, limited, and our freedom is contextualised. Our greatest latitude in exercising our freedom *lies in changing our attitude to what we meet*. This is just the kind of change we can hope for in a facilitated mediation.

It has been suggested that an avoidance of loss is at the root of disputes—the loss of the actualisation of one's values, assumptions, aspirations, and expectations. *The avoidance of loss is also the foundation for any conflict resolution.*

In a dispute, the parties seek to win everything and lose nothing; this is the hoped-for ideal. In a conflict, much as in life in general, we find that even though we may have done 'everything right', we are still confronted with loss and suffering. This reflects the premise that even our best intentions (as well as those that are not so virtuous) can produce results that are unexpected and undesirable.

The uncertainty and anxiety that this realisation engenders can give pause for thought. What one desires and aspires to may retain their value, but the *how* in terms of implementation may have to be reconfigured.

Again, as those involved reflect on and clarify the intentions that are impeded by virtue of the conflict, it may become apparent that some compromises and some losses may be tolerable in light of what can be realised; what is worth giving up to get something else?

What gets in the way of this recognition is that people in a contest often feel that they shouldn't be there; they are focused on the 'unfairness' of the situation.

'Fairness', along with 'justice' and 'responsibility', are common themes in disputes. These conditions are usually viewed as absolutes; it is black or white, totally fair or unfair, simply just or not, or 'their entire fault, not mine'.

This latter issue of fault, liability, or responsibility is one of the most frequently heard concerns in a dispute. It is often important to assign blame to an external person or source, not only so that one may be righteous, but also so that one's part in one's own suffering is denied; to be the source of one's own predicament is a difficult admission. If that is the case, then the basis for choice would appear to be erroneous, even if ethically sound, and uncertainty then has a foothold.

'Fairness' also has complex implications. If one is treated unfairly and is powerless to correct this disparity, one's expectations of self, other, world, and cosmos can suffer a critical blow; life is not supposed to be like this, as the actions and choices were well-intentioned.

Positioning at the commencement of a conflict is often rooted in moral and ethical certainties, according to the opponents involved; something or someone is indisputably wrong, and someone or something else is totally righteous. Human beings are drawn to these kinds of polarities, life and death being the prime example of what attracts and appals us. Such rigid, simplistic opposites seem to be easily identified, readily apparent; 'nothing complicated there' is the thought process.

But it is not a sustainable perspective; this view readily crumbles under closer inspection. But to accept that these values are not so clearly defined or applied in the messy context of real-life situations, in which I recognise that I too am the foil for the other's desires and aspirations, can rumble one's moral foundation to the core.

This discomfort is what often fosters reconsideration of one's position; the thought arises: 'If I am not completely justified, where can I—how can I—retain any moral high ground?' Or, in some cases, the concern will be for the advantage that lies in *appearing* to occupy the righteous position.

This can be in the form of reputational issues, in a public or commercial sense, but it is also certainly a concern for the maintenance of the expectations for self, others, world, and cosmos. Everyone is striving to create and maintain their world-view and the values of which it is comprised, and hoping to enlist the aid of others in making this so—or at least, in minimising the opposition to their intentions.

This model of human existence provides the 'common ground' between us all, including the mediator, the parties to the dispute, and the concerns of corporate entities and public organisations; we are struggling with the world and with each other for the same purpose, that is, to make existence align with our values.

An appreciation of these themes—e.g., fairness, responsibility, justice—that arise from many of the 'givens' outlined previously is itself a strategy for understanding and managing conflict. Exploration is the essential tool for unravelling any specific conflict, and it must be embedded in an attitude that respects the 'truth' of the other, although we might not agree with it; and the discoveries and realisations of both vulnerabilities and possibilities must be grounded in trust that these will not be exploited.

Chapter 13

Format, protocol, and process for facilitative mediation

The format described here offers a very flexible template for conducting mediation. The structure will be different for mediations that are assigned to one day, as is often the case in legal or commercial disputes, to those that that might take place over multiple sessions across a few days, as in family or community disputes.

For the aspects of the mediation format that are consistent with most situations, the rationale for maintaining these procedural elements will be clarified. However, it is imperative that the facilitator adopt a flexible approach to all aspects of the process, as this will allow a creative response to the people and the situations that are encountered.

This process should be as informal as possible, even if there is counsel present. Everyone in attendance should be referred to by name, even if they are representing an organisation. No one should be addressed as if they *are* the organisation (for example, the facilitator wouldn't invite 'the bank' to make a comment).

The one condition of almost all mediations is that of confidentiality; this includes 'without prejudice', if there is a legal case pending (WP simply means that anything said in the mediation cannot be used in court). The limits of confidentiality must be made clear at the start; clear contracting is an ethical obligation.

An additional condition of most mediations is that it is a voluntary arrangement; anyone is free to withdraw at any time.

Confidentiality encourages candour. The parties often need the mediator to understand just what is at risk for them, as well as why they feel justified in their demands.

Pre-mediation contact with parties is not always necessary or possible. The extent of the contact is also a matter of preference. It is advisable, at least, to ascertain who is expected to participate, and to communicate this information to everyone. Even this matter may be a

Format, protocol, and process 101

point of contention; the facilitation may well begin at this juncture if the parties are unhappy about who might attend.

In family mediation, it often happens that the facilitator does not personally meet those in attendance before the first gathering, nor is there much paperwork to read ahead of time. In legal or commercial mediations, there may be an abundance of documents, legal and otherwise, from lawyers as well as parties, and the mediator may or may not have telephone contact with the challengers. Depending on the approach the mediator takes, it may or may not be necessary to be apprised of the 'facts' beforehand. As was suggested previously, how the facts have been experienced is the vital information in understanding the dispute. This information is never in the paperwork; it is in what the individuals involved reveal in terms of their aspirations and values.

As always, it is best to enquire as to what their concerns are if they voice objections to anything proposed in the mediation arrangements. The facilitator may also have ideas about which and how many people are invited; although it is necessary to have decision-makers in attendance, it is best to remain flexible.

One-day mediation is a paradigm that can be useful in most contexts, with the exception of community disputes; these of necessity may take place over a number of days, and at domestic sites. The duration of the procedure should be clarified so that everyone knows how much time is allotted. As noted previously, time can be a favourable factor in the process.

In keeping with the approach to responsibility, it is crucial to bear in mind that the mediator is responsible for the process, that is, the procedure, and the parties are responsible for, and are the primary source of, the content.

Those that are intending to be part of the process need to be informed of the practical arrangements. There is an initial joint session with all involved, and then the mediator speaks to each 'side' in private sessions, which may be represented by multiple persons. If people are accompanied by counsel, friends, or family members, it is advisable to see them together in the private sessions.

There will be occasions when an initial joint session is not agreeable to one side or the other. Again, some flexibility is necessary, as is some diplomacy in managing the situation. If this is the case, the practicalities, and the issues of confidentiality and the role of the mediator, must be addressed in private sessions.

It is usually most effective if all those attending on the day meet in a joint session; this gives all involved an opportunity to offer an update or

102 Format, protocol, and process

a review of the matters at hand. How long this continues, and under what conditions, is largely at the discretion of the facilitator.

Rules of conduct is a matter that should be considered carefully by the facilitator. It should be noted that any behaviour that is proscribed may necessitate 'policing'. For example, if the mediator insists that people do not shout, when this occurs, how will this be managed without appearing punitive to one side or the other or even to both? It can be more effective to propose a policy of 'respect', though this may sound vague.

The facilitator should begin the joint session with an explanation of confidentiality, the voluntary nature of the process, and a description of the role of the mediator. It is imperative that the mediator repeat, from the pre-mediation discussions, that they are not adjudicators, and that their role is to assist all those involved to reach a resolution that is agreeable to all, at least to some extent.

Those in attendance are then asked, one by one, to address the group and give a brief summary of how they view the current predicament. Everyone must at least be given the opportunity to speak, even if they decline, which is, of course, their prerogative.

These sessions can be quite emotionally charged. It can be useful to allow the exchange to carry on until such time as the parties are ready to move to private sessions, or at the point where there seems to be a great deal of repetition.

Private sessions serve a number of purposes. They allow the party to explore their concerns without fear of revealing their vulnerabilities to the other side; this can lead to a disclosure as to their 'hidden agenda'.

The hidden agenda comprises the intentions and ambitions that are at the heart of the dispute. These may be revealed in total or in part— the story usually unfolds as the party gains trust in the mediator. These aspects of the story may also be 'hidden' from the person; by virtue of exploration, the values and intentions become clarified and re-prioritised.

This information will usually include the benefits and liabilities of settling on the day, or the hopes directed at a court hearing, if that is an option, or the intentions to remain intransigent.

It is not an absolute procedural rule to convene private sessions. It can happen that things are resolved in a prolonged joint session, or that the parties prefer to meet together for the entire process. Again, the mediator can be flexible in this regard.

However, in the accepting and receptive ambience provided by the facilitator, the client has the opportunity in the individual talks to explore their position without fear of exploitation or manipulation. A great deal of discovery occurs for those involved in these meetings in terms of what

Format, protocol, and process   103

is *really* important apart from the posturing that is evident in the common session.

It is imperative that in the early stages of this process, whether in joint sessions or private, the facilitator *refrains from asking about the desired outcome*. There is no reason for anyone to modify their position until they have had the opportunity to explore the possible losses and gains of the situation.

It is also possible to convene a number of private and joint discussions as the day progresses. This is a judgement call on the part of the facilitator, who is hopefully sensitive to the input of those involved.

If private meetings are the preferred format, there will come a time when the mediator will be requested to pass specific information to the other party. As these discussions are confidential, it is imperative that the mediator is absolutely clear as to the content of the message to be taken to the other side. And, when presenting this message, the mediator must articulate that they have been given permission to relay this specific message.

In this manner, the agreement can be 'built', one or two conditions and requests at a time. One of the most common messages requested for delivery is that of information, usually concerning motivation, which is either offered by one side or the other or is desired by one or both parties.

Confidentiality within this process must be strictly observed, as this supports the respect for those involved to find their own solution without the interference of a facilitator who thinks they know what needs to be communicated, agreed to, or acted upon.

This process is not linear; people 'move' in various directions. The mediator should bear in mind that in discovering vulnerabilities and possibilities, the parties will become defensive again at certain points and conciliatory at others.

It can also be effective to clarify what benefits can be gained by reaching an agreement on the day; these advantages can then be reviewed and repeated at strategic points. But these must originate with the parties, and it is equally important to consider the compromises or losses that might be incurred.

It is almost inevitable that at some juncture during the process, there will be a 'deadlock'. At this point, people often feel they have 'given up' enough of their original demands, they are frustrated with the process, and they may become entrenched in the current position.

It is advisable to allow a pause in the proceedings when this occurs; there isn't anything to *do* on the part of the mediator. What is usually happening is that those involved in the dispute are feeling the loss

104 Format, protocol, and process

attached to compromise; grief, anger, and disappointment may be dominant experiences.

The mediator may feel frustrated, and even dismayed, that the movement that may have taken place already has lost momentum. It is essential that the mediator recall, again, that this is not their problem. As noted previously, all conflicts come to an end, in one way or another, only to become part of another cycle of disagreement, dissent, and resolution in the form of defeat, triumph, or collaboration.

Most often, those involved regroup for further discussions. The mediator should remain steadfast, as there is certainly still hope at this point.

If the parties do arrive at an agreement, it is customary to commit this to writing as a group.

Not all mediated disputes come to an agreement on the day. However, it frequently occurs that in legal and commercial cases, there is a settlement reached before the court date. In family, workplace, and organisational disputes, it may happen that those who were party to the dispute have a deeper understanding of their difficulties; this may lead to informal experiments or collaborations in addressing the problems.

For the facilitator, it is also useful to remind themselves of their aim and purpose: to serve those involved and assist them in clarifying their desires and intentions and in developing the possibilities for a mutually agreeable resolution. Sometimes that agreement is to continue with the contrary positions they originally held.

Chapter 14

Ethical considerations for conflict and resolution

It is beyond the scope of this text to cover theories of ethics in any depth, even if the discussion were to be confined to existentialist thought. In this exposition, then, some fundamental ethical concerns relevant to conflict management and mediation will be presented in brief.

There has always been much debate about what differentiates morals from ethics. However, there seems to be some consensus that morals are personal values and ideals, while ethics are the codes for conduct that reflect, and are an extension of, the moral principles.

With that in mind, a review of some of the existential proposals discussed earlier in this text may shed some light on how these are relevant for understanding and managing conflict. To the extent that these proposals give rise to values, they can inform behaviour and practice.

Freedom, choice, and responsibility are issues that are regarded as fundamentals in existential thought and practise. Recalling also that life is grounded in relatedness, these aspects will all be manifest in how we are with each other, that is, in what kind of expectations and assumptions we have about the with-world in which we 'abide' (Heidegger 1993).

A much-quoted comment from Heidegger may provide some perspective (these are modes of being-with):

> solicitude has two extreme possibilities . . . it can . . . take away 'care' from the other . . . it can *leap in* for him . . . there is also the possibility of a kind of solicitude which does not so much leap in for the Other as *leap ahead* of him . . . (Heidegger 1993, p. 138)

To 'leap in' is to relieve someone of the burden of finding their own way and discovering their own values. Polt compares this to the teacher who provides students with answers to the questions to make it easier for them, but also perhaps to make themselves feel good about being helpful (Polt

106 Ethical considerations

1999). In such a scenario, the person who is the recipient of this 'help' can become dependent, even submissive, and loses the opportunity to be the author of their own life (not entirely, but it can be seriously impacted).

But to 'leap ahead' of someone is to open up possibilities for them. Polt compares this to a teacher who entices students with questions but allows them to find their own answers and discover their own priorities (Polt 1999). In this situation, one is in the service of another, without imposing an agenda, and with an open mind as to what is appropriate for the other person.

It may be apparent how these opposing modes of relatedness and intention can affect the exercise of choice and freedom. The givens cannot be displaced, but they can be subverted, or they can be authentically engaged with.

It is also important to note that often a person seeking help may *wish* to be relieved of the burden and blessing of choice and freedom. Responsibility has its drawbacks, and it would sometimes be a relief to be excused from these inevitabilities, or to know, with certainty, what *is* the 'right' choice. But to indulge such an (futile) attempt at avoiding responsibility would deprive the person seeking answers of the opportunity to creatively and authentically meet the challenge.

This is particularly relevant to any truly facilitative endeavour, including, of course, psychotherapy and mediation.

In hoping for a resolution to a dispute, one must maintain the naive stance. It is impossible to 'know' what is the best course of action for those involved, either for psychotherapy clients or for parties to a mediation. We can understand the concerns that are present for us all, but exactly how anyone will *respond to* or *engage with* the particulars of any given context is unpredictable. We, as the other, have only a partial understanding of their view; we can share their horizon only to a very limited extent.

By virtue of this limitation, we must in all humility, and perhaps with some relief, recognise that as a facilitator in any predicament, *it is not my problem and neither can it nor should it be my solution.*

If we respect and cherish the freedom of others, we cannot in good conscience impose a decision on someone else.

If we value and acknowledge our own freedom, even with its factical limitations, we must also recognise that no one *can* make the choice for us; even if we adhere to religious or cultural norms, it is in our power to reject these and accept the consequences.

In keeping with these proposals, and bearing in mind how the exercise of our freedom is an aspect of an authentic position, it may become apparent that to act ethically, one must choose which of one's values to actualise and how to do so; to refer one's decision to an exterior source of morals or ethics is an act of 'Bad Faith' (Sartre 1993). And here resides the risk that is inherent in all ethical and moral choices: we can never be sure that the choice we make will produce the results we are hoping for.

Additionally, therein lies the likelihood of ethical dilemmas: the realisation of one value becomes an impediment to that of another. More will be discussed about this common situation.

In terms of facilitated mediation, there are four principle arenas for ethical considerations: legal constraints, and one's responsibility to the process, to the parties, and to oneself.

Legal constraints are those that are specifically inscribed in law, as in the limits to confidentiality, as well as those parameters that are recognised as aspects of public policy, as in issues around child safety and public welfare.

However, a mediator also has responsibility to the process and to the people involved, and sometimes this extends to those who are not even present at the meetings, but implicated. Those involved have invested their time, money, and the hopes of a favourable outcome in this project, and these expectations should be respected, even if they are sometimes overly optimistic.

As an example of a dilemma, imagine that a facilitator is given the information that a low-level misdemeanour has taken place that is attached to the current dispute. It will be necessary to consider whether it is necessary to recuse oneself or to bring the process to a close, knowing that the parties may then be obliged to pursue an expensive, exposing, and disagreeable court case.

The mediator's responsibility to the parties is also manifest in the intention to *do the best that one can do*. It is a condition that cannot be qualified by the level of satisfaction of those involved; all those involved will experience varying levels of satisfaction, both during and after the process.

The fourth area of ethical consideration is the responsibility to oneself, which often overlaps with the other categories of responsibility. This attitude demands that the facilitator be aware of their biases and limitations, to the extent that this is possible, and be transparent about circumstances that would impact their impartiality. An example of this might be that a mediator declines to work with issues of animal mistreatment, as this is a concern that would affect their own psychological well-being as well as prejudice their participation.

108 Ethical considerations

Impartiality is an aspiration that is central to the practice of mediation, but one must be very careful about what is promised. It would be impossible to exist without one's own values and expectations, so the very best that can be hoped for is that the facilitator will be aware of their own prejudices, even as they are revealed during the process, and do their best to avoid imposing these on the person or the proceedings. It may be appropriate for the mediator to declare that they are impartial with respect to the outcome of the process, even if there is no agreement; this indicates that the responsibility for a resolution, or the lack of one, is firmly placed with the parties.

Even from these brief descriptions, it is probably obvious that any of these categories of responsibility could readily implicate another, resulting in an ethical dilemma.

Spinelli comments on this eventuality:

> the many dilemmas we are confronted with throughout life are not principally concerned with questions of right versus wrong but about *the choices* we make between actions that, in themselves, contain elements of both 'right' and 'wrong'. (Spinelli 1994, p. 124)

In terms of any facilitative project, the issue of power is always an ethical concern. As has been discussed earlier in this book, power is a dynamic; it is rarely total or absolute. Spinelli claims that all relationships are inherently imbalanced with respect to power (Spinelli 1994); perhaps it is more useful to consider, then, in what ways power is held, invested, yielded, or wielded in any given relationship. It can be readily demonstrated that, in most relationships, some form of power may be held or claimed by any of those who are involved.

The query that is particularly relevant for a mediator is whether or not it is their responsibility to 'address' power imbalances amongst or between the parties, but to address this condition is quite different to solving it, as if that were even possible. It is probably advisable, as well as ethical, to explore any disempowerment that is expressed, as this perspective may be open to review; it is also possible that the person feeling vulnerable may discover that they do have some leverage in ways that they may not have recognised. This is frequently illustrated in situations described as 'David and Goliath' scenarios; the outcome of that story is well-known. The point of this review of the power issue is that everyone has vulnerabilities, and the mediator should be aware that this is so, and that all parties are subject to threat that the loss of power and control provokes.

Ethical considerations 109

'Fairness' and 'justice' are also issues that are frequently expressed as goals of a resolution. However, these are very subjective evaluations; the question is always: fair to whom, or just in what sense? Again, the mediator should be sensitive to these aspects, but must appreciate that these ambitions may be accommodated in ways that are often not readily apparent, and indeed may never be revealed. It is paramount, therefore, that the facilitator brackets their own views on what might constitute what is fair or just; the parties involved are the experts on the problem, and on what may be necessary to serve their needs in this context.

And one should never underestimate the 'moral high ground'; if one party's ambition is to be seen as the magnanimous character, the other party may be happy to concede to this intention in order to have their own desires realised.

Finally, there is often some concern expressed amongst practitioners and parties concerning a dispute about 'safety'; most often, this concerns exposure of vulnerabilities that may then be exploited. If there is a fear of physical harm, this must be addressed with practical and contractual assurances, in much the same way that it would be in any context.

However, it is important to recognise that most people also want to feel safe with reference to their world-view, particularly in the sphere of self-concept; they hope to be perceived in the manner to which they aspire. If their intentions in this respect can at least be acknowledged, a level of acceptance and comfort is likely to ensue.

The quality of being-with described previously lends itself to the establishment of safety and trust. When a person's values are acknowledged, without opprobrium, they will feel *safer* than if they are provoked to defend them.

However, this safety is not absolute. A dispute situation is fraught with risk; this cannot, and should not, be assuaged. No amount of positivity can completely alleviate the challenges inherent in conflict or in life: in fact, these can be seen as opportunities for change, choice, and the exercise of agency.

Again, it is essential that the facilitator recognise these limitations to safety, and take them into account when describing the nature of facilitative mediation. Again, beware of making promises that cannot be kept.

These categories of ethical consideration overlap and impact each other; the distinctions made here are much murkier in an actual encounter. It is incumbent upon the facilitator to make 'judgement calls' at every turn. One should not be overly concerned about making mistakes, as they are rarely critical. It could be said that errors highlight the process as a very human endeavour, and that there are no absolute or final

Ethical considerations

answers to most of life's predicaments; neither is there anyone who holds the 'objective' truth or remedy to an inevitable cycle of conflict and resolution.

References

Heidegger, M. (1962) 1993 *Being and Time* (trans. J. Macquarrie and E. Robinson), Blackwell, Oxford.

Polt R. 1999 *Heidegger: An introduction*, UCL Press, London.

Sartre, J.P. (1943) 1993 *Being and Nothingness* (trans. H.E. Barnes), Routledge, London.

Spinelli, E. 1994 *Demystifying Therapy*, Constable, London.

Part II summary

The most important element in managing conflict, in the hope of a resolution of some kind, is one's attitude toward this constant cycle between the two events. It is understandable that conflict raises anxieties—we cannot know the outcome of the situation, but there are possibilities in engaging with it that are surrendered if one simply seeks to avoid it. To the extent that interpersonal conflict can be seen as an opportunity for communication and collaboration, it can yield creative solutions that promote authentic relations and living.

Conflict is always personal, as it implicates one's world-view. When the expectations, values, and ambitions that constitute our world-view are impeded in their realisation, we have emotional reactions to this event. Emotions, therefore, are the 'royal road to the world-view' in that they are indicative of which aspects are challenged or not acknowledged. Emotions are not the cause of behaviour; values that we seek to have actualised, and then preserved or maintained, are what we strive for, and are the basis for our choices, including behaviour.

Loss is an essential ingredient of conflict. Pending or future losses are what is being defended against, and one may feel that past losses demand justice, and sometimes retribution. The losses that are at the heart of any dispute are not just practical. It's never just about the money, or just about the liability; it is what the money, the liability, the apology, or the revenge *mean* in terms of one's concept of self, other, world, and cosmos.

The strategies of facilitative conflict management and resolution are aligned with existential thought. The source of both the conflict and the resolution is between or amongst the challengers; it is particular to them and to the current context. They must therefore be responsible for the agreement, as it must be a collaborative effort that serves their values.

It would deprive those involved of their responsibility if a facilitator were to impose their own agenda for a resolution. Such an imposition would be unethical, and lacking in respect and humility.

Trust between mediator and client in a dispute serves as bedrock for exploration and reflection. To the degree that parties can trust the mediator with the revelations of their vulnerabilities, even as they themselves are discovering them, the possibilities for cooperation between adversaries are increased.

Time is also a concern for those in dispute. Even when a person feels justified in their position, they still incur suffering; this is an experience that most seek to bring to a swift conclusion. The facilitator should take note of comments that indicate the desire to solve the situation in a timely fashion, and acknowledge that the loss of time spent on this dilemma is not retrievable. However, it is a juncture that warrants a reflective pause; it is an opportunity to consider what is lost, and what might be beneficial in coming to an agreement.

The opportunity to consider what possibilities one is abdicating when one says 'no' to one option, as well as the possible consequences of saying 'yes' to another option, serves to clarify that regardless of who holds the 'justifiable' position, everyone is at risk of some kind of loss. We are reminded that we cannot have it all, and that there is rarely, if ever, a 'win-win' outcome.

Dialogue is a quality of communication that can most effectively facilitate exploration of a person's world-view. In this attitude of listening and 'staying-with', the listener is in the service of the speaker; they bracket their own agendas and attempt to 'get alongside' the narrator in the hope of sharing, in some small part, the horizon of the speaker. This allows the speaker the chance to be heard by the facilitator, and also to hear themselves. This process allows for an unfolding of subjective truth; this truth is never final or total, but is relative to the current situation.

As the truth unfolds, perspectives alter and novel possibilities arise; the positions that are adopted in the first instance no longer seem so absolute. Throughout this 'tuning-in' phase, the speaker may become aware that even winning has its downside; it may incur losses that had not been previously acknowledged. At this juncture, the party begins to consider what they may be willing to give up or compromise in order to realise more important value and intentions.

When the party indicates they feel sufficiently heard, they may indicate that they are prepared to return to the subject of the current predicament and the need to find a resolution. The mediator should maintain

Part II summary 113

their patience and allow the party to consider what steps might be taken to 'move' things along.

The facilitator should not abandon the process of exploration and developing 'truth', and the practicalities of an agreement will be the fruit of these inquiries; the resolution is therefore 'built' piecemeal as priorities and intentions change.

Confidentiality is strictly maintained throughout the proceedings, until such time as one person or the other gives permission for a specific message to be presented to the other side; this prompts response, re-evaluation, and negotiation.

The development of an agreement is not linear; people become defensive and conciliatory by turn. This is to be expected as the benefits of settling, and the liabilities of maintaining the dispute, become clearer.

The ethical responsibilities of the mediator are evident in four main categories: legal constraints and public policy and responsibility to oneself, to the process, and to the parties.

Inevitably, there will be ethical dilemmas; these occur when one or more ethical principles necessitate the relegation of another. These contests can be experienced as losses; our certainty about truth and righteousness being absolutes can be seriously diminished, or our grounding can be shaken.

Not every facilitated mediation produces an agreement. But conflict always resolves, in one way or another, and the cycle of dispute and resolution continues.

When the contestants to a dispute allow for an exploration of the world-views which underpin their positions, it is likely that *something* changes, and sometimes this in itself is the positive outcome.

Case vignette 2

Unfair dismissal

The pre-mediation paperwork was not as onerous as usual: a single folder of printed emails and statements. I preferred not to read much about the cases (it made it easier to bracket what prejudices I might already have), but it was necessary to reply with all honesty to the inevitable query: 'Have you read the papers?'

Mrs. A, the head of faculty at Westfield primary school, had dismissed Mr. R, a teacher at the school, apparently without 'due process'. Mr. R had been frog-marched off the campus by a junior member of the teaching staff during lunchtime on a school day.

The matter had not yet been to a tribunal, and mediation had been strongly recommended by the Cavendish County Council; both parties had agreed to come to the mediation, presumably in the hope of avoiding costly and very public court proceedings.

We agreed to have one-day mediation, and the contract that outlined the parameters of the process had been signed by all in attendance. It had been agreed that legal counsel and union representatives would be excluded on this occasion. It was understood that this process would be entirely confidential, within certain legal restrictions; that attendance was voluntary; and that what was disclosed during the day would not be admissible in court, should it go that far. All parties in attendance had authority to settle should an agreement be reached.

I had some experience of workplace mediations, and I was always struck by how similar they were to family situations: an array of hurt feelings, misunderstandings, and inadequate communication. I was also aware that it was likely that there was a whole lot more to the story than was in the pre-mediation documents, but this too was common; the real nature of the dispute was never represented in the papers, but between or amongst the people involved.

116　Case vignette: Unfair dismissal

I was a bit nervous. Recently I had seemed to feel more impatient with conflicts that were so obviously a result of self-righteousness and delusion, but I did understand why people refused to listen or communicate directly; being 'wrong', even partially, is anathema to so many. And to say 'I'm sorry', an effective and inexpensive an offering as it is, seems to be an intolerable gesture for some.

I set aside these musings for the moment and reminded myself, 'This is not my problem'.

My aim was to do the best that I could and demonstrate my trust in the process: to maintain my impartiality (that is, not act on my own prejudices, but note them) and to bear in mind that the resolution for this dispute belonged to those involved, who were, in fact, the experts on the problem. I hoped for an agreement, but the quality of my contribution did not depend on it.

I saw this occasion as an opportunity for facilitated communication between the people here, and a possible agreement that would serve as many interests and values as possible, at least to some extent.

The three of us convened for a joint meeting on the morning of our day together.

'I'm not sure why I'm here . . . I have the legal and moral high ground here; there really isn't much to discuss. This could all be settled in court!' This was Mr. R's remark even as we all took our seats after brief introductions in the reception hall.

Mrs. A responded, 'You see how he is . . . self-righteous to the end! And the end is in sight, I tell you!' She matched his irritation in her comment, and sat down heavily on the armchair provided. Mr. R sat adjacent to her, and I had a third chair, forming a triangle amongst us.

These were typical openings to the very first meeting; each wanted to position themselves as the 'correct' and 'justified' party.

I thanked them both for their willingness to engage in the process, and stated that they would each have equal opportunity to elaborate on their points.

This was usually an important and fruitful stage of the day: the three of us together, implying that we were working as a team, although it felt like a contentious relationship for the moment. This was also the first chance they had had to speak to each other since the actual event of the dismissal. It was necessary for them both to see and hear the depth of the distress that was occurring.

It was also an opportunity for Mr. R and Mrs. A to consider me, who I was, and how I might handle this meeting with reference to my declared impartiality.

I explained my role as a facilitator, and that I in no way would be making judgements as to the 'truth' or 'righteousness' of their perspectives; I was there in the hopes of helping them to come to an agreement that would be at least somewhat more satisfactory than the other apparent options.

I then asked Mr. R to give his perception of the situation that we were here to consider.

'Can you imagine? I have been an educator at that school for more than ten years! How could she treat me like that, and so publicly! No sense of appropriate behaviour or respect! It just shows how hysterical and punitive she is . . . she is on shaky ground, my lawyer tells me . . . no correct procedure followed, we have a strong case . . . she should beware . . .'

Mr. R directed his comments to me until he issued the threat, which he spoke directly to Mrs. A.

Mrs. A seemed unconcerned about his warning. She sat calmly, her arms crossed across her chest as Mr. R made his statement. She then looked to me as she made her position clear.

'Listen to him; he thinks he is above it all. He thinks because of his long-term contract, he can get away with anything . . . he doesn't know who he's dealing with—although he should! Does he really believe that I would allow him to treat other members of our staff with such reprehensible disregard, with such inappropriate—' She broke off in anger and frustration.

From Mr. R's comments, I understood at this point that he was advising us of the strength of his legal position, but also that he was angry with the disrespect he had been shown by how the dismissal actually took place; it was this threat to his status as a respected member of the faculty that really grated. He subsequently resorted to undermining the behaviour of Ms. A, attributing it to hysteria and the intent to punish.

Mrs. A responded by charging him with arrogance and a lack of understanding with respect to her role and duties to her staff. From her point of view, he didn't really appreciate the lengths to which she would go to put a halt to his inappropriate behaviour.

Already, the anger displayed revealed some shared values: they were both faced with either a past loss or a pending one with reference to their self-concepts and to the profiles of themselves as they wished to be perceived.

The story, as I understood it, was that Mr. R had been dismissed from his position as history teacher at the school, on the basis that there had been a number of reports that he had been obviously severely hung-over when he arrived at school. Additionally, he had made sexual advances,

118 Case vignette: Unfair dismissal

under the influence of alcohol, to some female members of staff at the last two school fundraisers which had taken place in the early evening. These incidents had been seemingly out of character, as they had occurred only in the last year; up until that time, he had been a model, if aloof, constituent of the teaching team.

Mrs. A claimed that there had also been a number—three, to be exact—of unexplained and unexcused absences on the part of Mr. R; this demonstration of 'deteriorating' behaviour was exacerbated by the recent events at staff meetings and had 'forced' Ms. A to take some dramatic action.

Mr. R contested these stories, and asserted that the absences were taken as sick leave, although this wasn't documented, and that the scenarios described by Mrs. A were 'just a bit of harmless fun' meant to 'spice up' the otherwise dull social aspect of the meetings; no one had objected at the time.

I proposed that I would see Mr. R for the first private session, and I escorted Mrs. A to her own room.

I returned to the room Mr. R occupied on his own now, and was surprised to find him calmly sipping from a cup of hot chocolate.

His demeanour was much quieter now, but he seemed to be controlling, with some difficulty, a mounting irritation.

I invited Mr. R to elaborate further on the situation as he saw it.

'Mrs. A is a very disappointed woman, and she's taking it out on me.'

I waited to hear more.

'You women are all alike . . . first you flirt, make it all seem so acceptable, so—soft, so desirable, so winning . . .' He was sneering as his comment trailed off.

I was already bristling. I seriously disliked being 'lumped in' with all women; it was de-personalising, and a strategy commonly used as a defence against a more genuine relationship. I was very aware of my irritation, but decided to keep it in check for the time being. I was very interested in where this might be going.

Although his tone was even, his cynicism was evident, as was his simmering anger. What was the threat? I wondered.

'Push, pull, that's how you play it. A little something to keep a man interested, and a lot of grief to keep him at a distance . . . it's controlling and effective.'

'It sounds like you've had some experience of this strategy firsthand, Mr. R. Would you like to say more about it?'

I felt this was the right probe, as this was an issue that clearly had implications both for the dispute and for the relationship with me.

I wanted him to choose the direction, but I knew I would probably revisit the challenge to my non-judgemental proclamations in the introduction.

'Who can I trust? Mrs. A, or Helen, as I know her, is certainly not to be trusted; she has a skewed sense of fairness, and people, or at least I, am not much more than a convenience that is used when it suits her purpose. How can she just discard me, an educator with a sterling record, and a man, who was desperate for affection, and for the chance to . . .'

The story Mr. R told was one of unrequited love for Mrs. A, who had at first welcomed his advances, then rebuffed them without an explanation or excuse. This situation had affected their working relationship and Mr. R's performance; he had taken to occasional binge drinking, which left him hung-over and sometimes unable to attend to his teaching obligations. He felt that it was unfair and uncaring that she had taken action against him without even making a personal enquiry as to his well-being, which is what 'would be expected' if any other member of staff was in distress.

Additionally, he had made sexual advances to other female members of staff in an effort to 'show her' that she wasn't the 'only game in town', and the offended women had complained to Mrs. A. Mr. R was somewhat sheepish in making this revelation, but also steadfast in his assertion that he was 'encouraged' by the female co-workers; besides, he thought that everyone understood that it was just a bit of fun.

'So, Mr. R, from your point of view, you were sincere in your affections for Mrs. A, which were welcomed at first, and then withdrawn, without explanation, which left you angry and confused. And then, to put her in her place, so to speak, you turned your attentions in public to other women, but with too much force, shall we say . . . is that about right? And you believe, if I understand your comments, that you were dismissed unfairly, and that this was more a consequence of the failed relationship than your actual performance as a teacher?'

'Educator; I prefer the title of "educator"', he replied somewhat sullenly.

There was a short pause, and then he stated:

'You can see my point . . . but . . . can a woman ever really see the truth in a situation where the accusers are her own kind?'

This was the juncture at which I knew I had to address the implication of bias.

'Listen, Mr. R, I can understand that you have concerns regarding my claim of impartiality in this situation. I have never found it helpful to simply suggest that someone 'just trust me', so, instead, I would say that it certainly would not be effective for me to show favour to one side or the other, as this would most likely undermine the process of mediation.

120 Case vignette: Unfair dismissal

I can say that if you discern any demonstration of bias on my part, please bring it to my attention, and we can discuss it right there and then. Does that help at all?'

I left it to him, as I knew he would probably consider it further.

I understood that Mr. R was anxious about being exploited or manipulated if Mrs. A and I were to collude. The expression of his vulnerability was already an indication that he wanted to, and needed to, have some confidence in Helen and me, and in the process.

He agreed that he would be candid if he felt uncomfortable during the day's discussions, and I suggested we conclude our first session together. As I said this, he raised his hand to pause my comment, and interjected:

'I really want to be rid of this mess today. Even though I am told I have a good case, in terms of how the dismissal was handled, going to a tribunal is not an option . . . it's embarrassing, to say the least. And by the way, please call me Frank; it seems right, as you asked us to call you Karen.'

I was curious about this aversion to the tribunal, but I assured him we would have further opportunity to talk again, reminded him that everything he had said was confidential, and excused myself.

I felt that the final comment, an expression of both desperation and intent, and possibly a hint of vulnerability, indicated that he trusted me, a little bit anyway, at this point. It was a start.

Mrs. A seemed to be seated comfortably when I returned to her room. She had brought along a book to read, as I had explained there might be intervals when she would be on her own, and she had made use of the drinks vending machine.

In much the same way as I had issued the invitation to Frank, I asked her to tell me what was important for her with respect to the current dilemma.

'Please, call me Helen. I am fine with you, but I didn't want Frank to sound too . . . familiar. I want, *must* actually, maintain some decorum in front of him . . .'

Helen gave an account of how Frank had been absent from his duties three times in the last few months without a credible excuse, and reviewed the stories about him being intoxicated at the fundraisers and 'making a fool of himself' with the female staff.

'He was previously a model teacher . . . we have all had some sympathy for him, as his wife left him some years ago, and he has always seemed like a lost soul . . . that aside, this behaviour cannot go on; I have my reputation to protect, as well as that of the school, and it is my responsibility to maintain a professional and amicable atmosphere

Case vignette: Unfair dismissal   121

amongst all our personnel . . . it's nothing personal, it's just a necessary, and important, part of my job . . . which by the way, I've been doing for well over ten years now.'

Helen looked at me briefly before returning her gaze to her tea.

'How has all this affected you, Helen? I can hear that you do have some sympathy for Frank, but cannot tolerate any further behaviour as has occurred recently . . .'

'Well, yes, of course, Frank is obviously troubled, but he has no right to take it out on his colleagues! I've suggested he get some professional help . . .'

We paused. I allowed us both time to think about what had been said. I recognised that Helen hadn't answered my question, but thought it best to let it rest for a moment.

'I hope he is not going to be pig-headed about this. I know he has, and I have, been advised that he has a strong case for unfair dismissal, but a tribunal is so public . . .'

'And time-consuming', I added.

'Well, yes, time better spent supporting the advances and reputation of our institution . . . but I can't quite forgive him for this mess . . . he will absolutely have to apologise, publicly, without ambiguity, and the sooner the better!'

Helen banged her cup on the table. The sound surprised us both, and tea spilled onto the floor.

'I'm angrier than I realised!' she exclaimed.

'What is it exactly, Helen, that so angers you? Can you be specific?'

'Well, wouldn't you be? He's threatening the reputations, and the well-being, and the community of colleagues, of me and my staff—and of Westfield, of which I am known to be very protective!'

She took a deep breath, then:

'Frank is such an idiot. If only he had talked this out with me . . .'

This statement erupted from her. Anger, the threat of loss, and some confusion as to how she could reconcile ambivalent feelings and intentions were the core issues at this point.

'I'm really not sure how I would feel in your situation, Helen, but please tell me more about your own concerns . . . and remember this is all confidential, unless you decide that you wish me to communicate something specific to Frank.'

Helen sat back in her chair and seemed to reflect on her predicament.

I wasn't sure where the discussion might take us now. I wasn't worried that Helen was angry, or that she would continue to be, but I suspected there was something more to her dilemma.

122 Case vignette: Unfair dismissal

Helen went on to reveal that she had at one point encouraged Frank in his expressions of affection for her. She too was lonely, her husband had passed away some years previously, and she felt that her 'charms were fading' and that there might not be much more opportunity to create a loving and committed relationship.

This budding romance held many problems. It was a policy that staff should not become personally involved with each other. There had been some queries raised as to Helen's preferential treatment of Frank amongst the teachers. There had been veiled references to this subject in staff meetings, although the affair had apparently remained a secret. Helen was worried about the repercussions, for them both, should this news become public.

But what really bought the situation to a dramatic turn was when Frank, under the influence of a great deal of wine, had confessed to Helen that his new indulgence had become increasingly expensive, and he had considered other means of income.

When a couple who had two children enrolled in the school came to him with concerns about their children's exam results, which would affect their application to a new school, Frank offered to 'improve' the test marks for a 'small cash donation' that would be passed on to his favoured, though unnamed, charity.

Helen probed, tentatively, for further details of this event; Frank declined to elaborate. It left Helen wondering if the episode had actually taken place, or whether Frank was testing her loyalty to him in concocting the story.

In any event, Helen felt compromised by the account, whatever his intention, and promptly informed Frank that their relationship was well and truly over.

Helen inferred that the parents in question were under no delusions as to the exact nature of this transaction: she was aware of a family that were seeking to relocate to a new county and were hoping to enrol their twin boys in a prestigious school. However, there was, at present, no certainty that this occurrence as related by Frank had actually taken place.

I understood at once that this posed an ethical dilemma for Helen, and for Frank, as well as for the school, and possibly for me.

I decided that it would be wiser to push this responsibility back to Helen; we might have to work this out together.

I suggested:

'We can revisit this issue when you have considered it further, and you can decide what your options might be . . .'

I stopped there, and continued after Helen had nodded in assent.

Case vignette: Unfair dismissal   123

'So, you are really upset with Frank because he has jeopardised your professional standing and credibility, and his actions have left you feeling compromised. You did have some strong feelings for him, but . . . well, it sounds like you are hurt and disappointed with his behaviour both personally and professionally.'

I felt this last comment was more than was stated, but I thought it would be refuted if I really had misinterpreted the feelings that had been aired.

Helen was tearful but still irate.

'Yes, that about sums it up. Now what do I do? If this goes to a tribunal, the consequences could be very serious . . . I am so caught up in the middle, and it's a mess!'

She took a deep breath, and then commented:

'You know, I haven't said this to anyone before, but it is one of the few times in my whole life that I've done something I'm—ashamed of!'

Again, if this had been therapy, I would have explored the repercussions of this disclosure; with respect to the mediation, I suspected this novel awareness, this appreciation of guilt with reference to the breach of her own moral code, would have consequences for the process.

I thanked Helen for her candour, and expressed that I understood this was a difficult situation for her: she had multiple concerns and responsibilities, and it would be difficult to manage the various ethical, personal, and professional aspects that had been raised.

I took some time between sessions to review the process thus far. I was very aware of the common ground that the two shared: they were both compromised by ethical dilemmas, were both concerned for their professional and personal reputations, had both demonstrated some level of regret, and were both highly motivated to settle in mediation.

In the following private sessions, it came to pass that Helen, by virtue of her recognition of her own fallibility, developed some empathy for Frank, although she condemned his behaviour; she felt that he could and would regain his position as a valued member of faculty under certain conditions.

This intent for and about Frank was passed across to him, with Helen's express permission; it softened his attitude toward the situation, and he allowed me to communicate his response that he was 'quite prepared' to consider her suggestions. He also added that he still held Helen 'in high regard', and appreciated that she too was in a predicament.

Subsequent to a few more exchanges, passed through me, the parties were prepared to come to some arrangement.

Helen demanded an apology, in writing, to the members of staff that had complained of Frank's advances and another to the school personnel

124 Case vignette: Unfair dismissal

in general for his unacceptable behaviour. Frank was also referred to a therapist to help him deal with his issues, for a period of one year.

Frank never confessed to the circumstances of the bribe; as I was not at liberty to divulge the story Helen related to me, it was never corroborated. Helen felt that it was better left undisclosed and unexplored, as she subsequently came to suspect it was a fiction created by Frank to compromise her position and to make her complicit in his arrangements. Helen also recognised that such an event could compromise the integrity of the entire school as well as her own.

Frank accepted the terms of Helen's offer, and also insisted that other than the apologies, the conditions would be kept confidential. Frank also requested that his absences be recognised as legitimate, and that the past events not be recorded in his performance review, nor affect his contract in any way.

These terms were confirmed and written into a formal agreement. The Council and the union representative were informed that a settlement had been reached, but were not advised of the particulars.

Frank also expressed, in a final joint session with the three of us, that he too was greatly ashamed of his behaviour, particularly with respect to Helen, and that he would hope to regain her respect, if not her affection.

Reflections

Helen and Frank were both suffering, albeit from circumstances of their own making.

They both held regrets, and felt that their expectations of themselves, and the expectations of their colleagues, had not been met; they were angry with themselves for compromising the manner in which they hoped to be perceived by others, as well as their self-concepts, which had been also tarnished.

They both realised that what seemed like very private behaviour did in fact have repercussions for their wider professional and social profiles and reputations.

Helen seemed to gain a deeper understanding of her own needs and wants, and was determined to review her personal aspirations and hopes in connection with her own behaviour and choices. Her professional status was maintained, and she was grateful that her many years of dedication would not be besmirched.

Frank was in effect shocked at his own conduct, and discovered that he didn't 'know' himself quite as well as he thought. Where there were hidden depths of disillusionment and despair, there might also be unrecognised strengths and possibilities.

Frank was also relieved not to be cast as 'the villain of the piece', as he put it; he deeply appreciated the graciousness of Helen's attitude, and was moved to use his therapy to address a number of issues that might be affecting his ability to relate and to care for others.

There were moments when I was uncertain as to how this might work out, if at all, but I did feel that they made good use of the opportunity to understand their situation and themselves—not an easy assignment, as it often requires a shift in one's perspective, a shift that can resonate throughout the world-view. As is often the case, Helen and Frank both moved from a 'blaming' position to one that acknowledged their own responsibilities in creating the dilemma.

I felt that I managed some quality of dialogue, at least an attitude that allowed some trust to flourish. I was not as comfortable with Frank as I was with Helen, but I didn't overcompensate for this; I kept it my awareness, always considering how it might be affecting my being-with them both.

Initially, I really wasn't sure if they would be able to come to an amicable arrangement, but I also realised it would be counterproductive to try to move it along any faster than it was developing.

The agreement came in small increments, and started with communications about feelings and intentions; the practicalities were a consequence of these seemingly modest expressions.

The ethical dilemma was a typical example of competing responsibilities to the process, to the parties, to public policy, and to oneself. It was decided that, as the story was uncorroborated, the duty to the parties and the process were best served by avoiding further inquiries for the time being. Helen felt it was imperative to maintain the school's reputation, and that the greater good would be served by leaving the incident undisclosed; she took it upon herself to keep a close watch on Frank's activities in general.

I felt this was appropriate, though not entirely satisfactory, as is often the case with ethical concerns that fall into a 'grey' area; I too felt that the event was unlikely to be repeated, but of course, there were no guarantees.

The therapeutic effects were with reference to the world-views. The concept of self, for Helen and Frank, was shaken, as they had not lived up to their aspirations in this regard; the expectations about how others should and would behave had been unfulfilled; the assumptions about how the world would be fair and forgiving were challenged; and the cosmological attitude that good intentions always provide positive results for good people was reconsidered.

To suggest that changes in the world-view are therapeutic is not to propose that they are easily endured; such modification can provoke the anxiety that is concomitant with uncertainty, and it is necessary to note that not all such alterations will be welcomed or regarded as 'positive'. However, as discussed previously, anxiety is the cost of freedom, choice, and responsibility: the burdens and blessings of human existence.

Conclusion

Conflict can be a deeply disturbing experience. We may think we know how we will respond, but in the moment, it can all be otherwise. If the threat is extreme, we may behave in ways, both positive and negative, that we never thought would even occur to us.

Such an event can shake the very core of our world-view. We may question our views on ourselves, others, the world, and the cosmos. We can be left with a feeling that nothing is as it seems; we may have to do some reconstruction of the assumptions and aspirations that allow us to navigate our way through the world with some semblance, or illusion, of safety.

However, and thankfully, such crises are infrequent. The kind of interpersonal conflict addressed in this book is the more common altercation experienced and witnessed in everyday life. However, it should be noted, as proposed in this discussion, that even such a modest occurrence can also disrupt one's world-view, and call into question some or all of what we believe to be 'true'.

In such circumstances, we also become aware of the limits of our understanding, and of those of 'truth'; in fact, we may become aware that many 'truths' are not total, final, or even entirely communicable. This is due in part to the modifications in our own world-views, the kinds of alterations that lend themselves to novel perspectives and more inclusive horizons. From these new vantage points, we may see different options for managing our dilemmas.

'Other people' often seem to be the source of our troubles. They can directly inhibit our aims and/or disparage our intentions and desires. In either case, we are faced with a threat, either to our practical projects or to the values and aspirations reflected in our world-view. What is particularly grating about this scenario is that it seems that those who oppose our endeavours are doing so willingly, with little regard for our

128 Conclusion

own priorities. In fact, we are often amazed that someone, especially one who we think knows us well and agrees with our perspective, takes a completely contrary view on the circumstances.

It is such assumptions as these, unmined for intricacy or variability, that often function as a basis for a serious misunderstanding.

Such threats to our projects will always illicit an emotional response. This may not be immediately detectable, but the level of response, and the manner, will be commensurate with the investment we have in the source of the threat.

If we wish to maintain a relationship with the person challenging us, or if our purposes are more important than 'winning' the contest, we may be amenable to collaboration and compromise. In order for this to happen, we will usually need to allow for a deeper understanding of the Other's position as well as our own. It is often the case that those involved have not considered the many contradictions in, and consequences of, their initial position.

The initial position, even if qualified as 'offensive', is always in defence of a pending loss. The loss, and its significance, is the foreground of the clash. Further consequences are relegated, until such time as a deeper inquiry can be launched or facilitated.

It is imperative that the aspects of the world-view that are implicated in any conflict are discovered and considered. To the extent that these can be acknowledged and served, there will be conciliation and cooperation; to the extent that these are denied and impeded, the contest will be hotly maintained, possibly even to the point of damage to or destruction of either or both parties.

To achieve the most beneficial outcome to a conflict, in terms of the least amount of loss and the most amount of gain, it is necessary that these elements are recognised and understood.

Reflection and dialogue can assist in discovering these for oneself; in so doing, we may realise that we hold competing and ambiguous values, and that most of what we want cannot be achieved alone.

Communication, careful consideration, and a certain amount of risk-taking are required to allow an Other to understand our priorities and their meaning for us. To disclose one's aspirations and intentions is to open oneself to the possibility of manipulation and coercion, but without this kind of exposure, we are less likely to achieve a resolution that attends to our deepest aspirations and intentions.

Although this endeavour harbours risks, it may be even more detrimental to seek to impose a settlement that denies or disregards the principles that are at the root of the dispute. Such an event depersonalises

Conclusion 129

those involved, and it is just this kind of dehumanisation that is a common complaint in conflict situations.

What is being promoted in this book is that conflict is sourced in subjective truth and private logic; it is this perspective that must be acknowledged and understood, at least to some extent. To the degree that these 'truths' can be acknowledged and implemented, the outcome of the challenge can be satisfying and productive—we might even say 'therapeutic'. Although complete satisfaction is certainly not guaranteed, what is likely is that one's perspective has been augmented, one's appreciation and understanding have been deepened, and the worst-case scenario has been avoided.

We discover what values and ambitions are being thwarted in any given contest by looking at the emotional expressions and communications. These may be subtle or overt, but those involved will communicate how they feel about the situation; they cannot help but be engaged in some way.

If we consider our own emotional responses to the circumstances, and to the quality of engagement with an Other, it is possible to discern in what way we are being blocked, undermined, or devalued. By virtue of the same inquiry, we may also discover what values have priority, and what possible options may be available in the service of realising at least some of our intentions, and at what costs.

It must be noted, though, that emotional expressions and awareness are not the aims of the process; they are the indicators of the values at stake.

In a comment that is relevant for both therapy and understanding what drives a conflict, Bugental offers this insight:

> Emotions . . . are similar to blood in surgery: both are inevitable as the work goes forward: both importantly serve a cleansing and function and foster healing; both must be respected and dealt with . . . and *neither is the point of the procedure.* (Bugental 1992, p. 113)

To ignore or distract from the emotional indicators is to waste the very valuable information they can provide.

In a conflict, what is usually sought is change. The possibility of change is inherently anxiety provoking, even when we can seemingly predict the results; the outcome may bear some semblance of what was hoped for or expected, but it also frequently bears unanticipated consequences, some of which may not be so appealing. As has been suggested, when change occurs, it is rarely a win-win situation.

130 Conclusion

May succinctly states:

Decision precedes knowledge. (May 1969, p. 87)

This is a fundamental reason why people resist change. It is difficult, if not impossible, to ascertain the 'right' choice, even based on past experience (the circumstances of which can never be exactly replicated anyway); we must choose armed only with limited comprehension and a hope of a desired outcome.

There can be an advantage, however, in anticipating that change must and will occur. In this respect, we can choose to make modifications in our attitude and behaviour; in this way, we may be able to mitigate the direction and impact of transformations.

These principles can be effectively demonstrated in the context of a facilitated mediation. In this model, an impartial third party provides a quality of listening and response that allows those involved to reveal and discover the aspects of their world-views as they are relevant to the dispute.

Although some skills are delineated here in this text, these must be embedded in an appropriate *attitude*; this is grounded in the existential phenomenological proposals outlined in this discussion. The aim and outcome of such an attitude are aligned with proposals around themes such as freedom, responsibility, and choice; the hoped-for resolution is one that is deeply personal for, and therefore clearly 'owned' by, those involved.

As the mediation process is one of 'facilitation', and not of coercion or 'objective' rationale, the distress and disappointment that is often the consequence of an imposed or coerced resolution is minimised. Again, the exercise of agency as described in the existential approach is a much more satisfactory experience; one feels that it is possible to have some effect on one's own situation.

The attitude that is described in some detail earlier in his text is one that aspires to a 'dialogical' engagement, a quality of being-with that puts aside technique in favour of 'a real encounter'. This approach eschews analysis and opts instead for understanding.

This understanding is in the service of the party, or the client, but it will by its very nature affect the facilitator as well.

The attitude is grounded in 'presence': an acknowledgement and appreciation of how we are all struggling with the same issues, as well as how these issues are experienced concretely and specifically by the person involved.

With respect to psychotherapy, May and colleagues suggest:

> *Presence* is not to be confused with a sentimental attitude toward the patient but depends firmly and consistently on how the therapist conceives of human beings. (May et al. 1961, p. 81)

The principle holds true for the mediator who seeks to conduct a facilitated resolution, as well as for anyone involved in challenging or difficult relations.

Mediation, as a form of alternative dispute resolution (ADR), seeks to return some semblance of power, control, and responsibility to those involved. It can provide opportunities for enhanced relationships, as well as a deeper understanding of oneself and others.

All conflicts will come to some kind of ending: things change or remain the same. The cycle is endless and inevitable. Hopefully, this exposition provides some insight into how this fact can be seen as an opportunity instead of an adversity.

References

Bugental, J.F.T. (1987) 1992 *The Art of the Psychotherapist: How to develop the skills that take psychotherapy beyond science*, Norton, New York.

May, R. 1969 *Love and Will*, Bantam Doubleday Dell, New York.

May R., Angel, E. and Ellenberger, H. (1958) 1961 *Existence*, Basic Books, New York.

Index

absolutism 43, 98, 99
acceptance 89–90
addiction 62, 63, 66, 69, 70
agency 17, 58, 87, 109; contingency 22; cooperation 81; existential approach 8, 130; inauthenticity 41
aggression 3, 10, 12, 79
agreement 3, 97, 103, 104, 113, 124, 125
alcoholism 62, 66
alternative dispute resolution (ADR) 73–4
anger 6, 79, 84, 104; family conflict case vignette 69, 71; unfair dismissal case vignette 117, 118, 121, 124
angst 20, 21–2
anxiety 1, 14, 21–2, 29, 126; about emotions 87; avoidance of conflict 79; choice and 34; facilitators 90; family conflict case vignette 71; human contact 36; loss and 98; plasticity of guiding principles 49; possibility of change 55, 129; self-concept 30; temporality 41, 43; transience 40
'a-partness' 20
apologies 74, 86, 121, 123–4
aspirations 2, 35, 55, 57, 87; actualisation of 84, 86; avoidance of loss 98; choice and 40; conflict resolution 73; cosmological level 3; defence against loss 59; disclosure of 128; experience of 'facts' 101; family conflict case vignette 70;

impediments to 18, 79; recognition of 37, 96; trust 95; unfair dismissal case vignette 124, 125; values and 17; *see also* world-views
assumptions 23, 87, 95, 105; avoidance of loss 98; bracketing one's 47, 90, 91; emotions 83, 84; mediators 108; mistaken 48, 70; threats to 79; unfair dismissal case vignette 125; world-views 2, 27–30, 46, 49, 55, 57, 73, 77; *see also* expectations
attitude 130
authenticity 42–3, 81
avoidance of conflict 79–80

Bad Faith 36, 41, 107
Barnes, Hazel 38
Barrett, W. 34
Becker, Ernest 43, 78
being 33–4
being-for-others 18, 37
being-in-the-world 15–16, 17, 23, 34–5, 45, 84
being-with-others 14, 17–18, 53, 75, 90, 109, 130
bias 48, 70, 90, 107, 119–20
Binswanger, Ludwig 27
blame 43, 66, 72, 98, 125
body and mind 24
Boss, M. 25
Buddhism 34
Bugental, J.F.T. 20, 129

Cannon, B. 37
care 40, 42

Index 133

Cartesian dualism 24
change 1, 8–9, 20, 24–5, 58–9; anxiety evoked by 55, 129; as constant of human existence 47; existential psychotherapy 81; family conflict case vignette 71; inevitability of 96; resistance to 130; transience 40; uncertainty and 80; world-views 31
chaos 48, 79
choice 1, 8–9, 15–16, 20, 36–7, 43; anxiety as the cost of 126; changeability 31; changing one's world-view 48; consequences 57; ethical issues 105, 107; facilitative resolution 75; facticity 39–40; family conflict case vignette 70; freedom and 21, 42, 55; Heidegger 17; re-choosing 30, 32; relatedness and intention 106; resistance to change 130; responsibility of 49, 52, 106; self-actualisation 34; time and 40–1; values and assumptions 31
clarification 9, 10, 102, 104
cognition 84, 87
Cohn, H.W. 8, 17, 24, 43, 51, 75, 81, 92
collaboration 17, 38, 59, 80–1, 104; amenability to 128; in dialogue 90; family conflict case vignette 72; trust needed for 95; see also cooperation
common ground 37, 48, 70–1, 72, 99
communication 6, 9, 14, 55; dialogical attitude 53; emotions 129; mediation 74; skills 2, 90, 92; see also dialogue
compensation 12, 43
compromise 3, 58, 81, 97, 103–4, 112, 128
confidentiality 100, 107, 113; family conflict case vignette 65; joint sessions 102; private sessions 101, 103; unfair dismissal case vignette 115, 121, 124
conflict, attitudes about 77–81
consciousness 45–6
contingency 22, 29, 45, 46, 48, 54
contracts 70, 71, 115

Cooper, M. 15
cooperation 3, 35–6, 37, 79; family conflict case vignette 69; possibility for 81, 112; see also collaboration
cosmos 28, 48, 111
counselling 8

Dasein 33–4, 40
deadlock 103–4
death 1, 15–16, 19, 20, 25; care and 40, 42; Heidegger 17; temporality 59
defensiveness 6, 12, 14, 49, 89
demands 37
de-personalisation 9, 12, 118, 128–9
description 47, 49, 90, 91
'de-sedimentation' 30
Deurzen-Smith, E. van 8, 27
dialogical attitude 2, 53, 55, 130
dialogue 13, 14, 53–7, 81, 128; collaboration in 90; dialogical engagement 94; exploration of world-view 112; silence in 93; see also communication
Dilthey, Wilhelm 51
disrespect 117
domination 37
dualism, Cartesian 24

Eigenwelt 27
embodiment 1, 19, 20, 24, 71, 84, 87
emotions 2, 83–8, 91, 111, 129; embodiment of 71; emotional reactions 12–13; world-views 30
empathy 54
engagement 13, 14
epoché 47
ethical issues 100, 105–10, 113, 122, 123, 125
evaluative mediation 74–5
existence 33
'existential givens' 1, 5, 8–9, 15–16, 19–25, 34, 57
existential psychotherapy 1, 5–10, 15, 43, 47, 77, 81
existentialism 1, 6–8, 15–18, 87, 130; conflict and collaboration 80–1; emotions 83; facilitative resolution 111; knowing 53

134 Index

expectations 2, 18, 29, 46, 57, 77; about others 28; avoidance of loss 98; change of intention 55; ethical issues 105; family conflict case vignette 63, 70, 71, 72; gender bias 48; impediments to 111; maintenance of 99; self-concept 30; uncertainty 49; unfair dismissal case vignette 124, 125; unfairness 99; *see also* assumptions; world-views

exploration 3, 89, 99, 102, 112, 113; emotions 85, 86–7; existential psychotherapy 8; naiveté 58; phenomenological method 90–2

facilitative resolution 9, 73–5, 100–4, 109, 111–13, 130–1
facticity 39–40, 42
facts 7, 46, 58, 91, 101
fairness 98, 99, 109
family mediation 61–72, 101
fear 14, 83
freedom 1, 9, 15–16, 20, 21, 22; anxiety as the cost of 126; authenticity 42; as burden and blessing 31; changeability 31; to choose 55; contextualisation of 98; curtailing of 39; 'dizziness' of 46; ethical issues 105; family conflict case vignette 70; impediments to 77; others as threat to 35; relatedness and intention 106; time and 41; world-views 57
Friedman, M. 6, 15
the future 39, 41–2, 70, 85, 96, 97
Gadamer, Hans-Georg 23, 51, 53, 54
Good Faith 36, 81
groups 13
guilt 17, 67, 80, 123

Harding, M. 23
Heidegger, Martin 6, 17, 25, 33–4; anxiety 21; emotions 83; hermeneutics 51; solicitude 105; time 40, 41–2
hermeneutics 17, 23, 51–6, 58, 92
'hidden agenda' 102
horizontalization 47

human condition 6, 18
Husserl, E. 47

Iacovou, S. 81
impartiality 11, 74, 107–8, 116, 119
inauthenticity 41, 42
incredulity 12
intentionality 46, 84, 106
interpretation 46, 58, 92–3; hermeneutics 51–6, 92

Jaspers, Karl 93
joint sessions 101–2, 103
justice 16, 98, 99, 109

Kafka, Franz 6
Kierkegaard, Søren 6, 16
knowing 53
knowledge 51, 52, 130

lack of control 12, 30
Langdridge, Darren 47, 50
language 1, 20, 23–4; family conflict case vignette 71; Gadamer on 53, 54; Heidegger 17
legal issues 100, 101, 107
Lindberg, R. 37
listening 14, 55, 92, 112
'the look' 35, 38
loss 25, 32, 43, 55, 111, 112; avoidance of 98; change and 58–9; compromise 103–4; defence against 59, 128; emotions 85; threat of 12–13; transience 40
love 18, 35, 58, 86

Macquarrie, J. 7, 33, 41, 84, 93
manipulation 5, 10, 95, 128
May, Rollo 2, 6, 16, 130, 131
meaning 20, 22, 46
meaninglessness 1, 20, 22, 29, 31
mediation 3, 14, 98; definition of 73–4; ethical issues 107–10; evaluative 74–5; facilitative 2–3, 74, 75, 100–4, 109, 111–13, 130–1; family conflict case vignette 61–72; unfair dismissal case vignette 115–26
Merleau-Ponty, Maurice 6, 40
mind and body 24

Index 135

mistrust 80
misunderstanding 5, 53
Mitwelt 27
moral high ground 42, 99, 109, 116
morality 17
mortality 25, 59
movement 86–7, 96, 112–13

Nagarjuna 34
naiveté 52, 58, 91, 92, 106
needs 9–10, 13
negotiation 13
Nietzsche, Friedrich 6, 16–17
noema 46
noesis 46
non-being 41

objectivity 7, 11
one-day mediation 101, 115
ontology 16, 34
organisations 11
the Other 33, 35–6, 111, 128; assumptions and values about others 28, 48; dialogue with 53; mistrust of 80; quality of engagement with 129; resonance with 57; respecting the truth of 99; solicitude 105

perception 45, 46, 49
personal, emphasis on the 9, 11, 14, 35, 55
phenomenology 23, 30, 45–50, 51, 130; emotions 84; Heidegger 17; phenomenological method 47–8, 49, 58, 90–2
Polt, R. 22, 83, 105–6
power 87, 108, 131
pre-mediation contact 100–1
presence 130–1
'private logic' 13, 27, 30, 32, 57, 73, 86, 129; see also world-views
private sessions 101, 102–3
psychoanalytical model 52

Randolph, P. 27, 74, 75
rapprochement 5
reality 45, 47, 49
re-appraisal 46
reason 84, 87

re-choosing 30, 32
reciprocity 37, 53, 81
reconciliation 17, 64
regrets 71, 72
relatedness 17, 19–20, 35, 36; conflict as inevitable aspect of 81; ethical issues 105; exercise of choice and freedom 106; facilitative resolution 75; trust 96
relationships 19, 36, 58, 108
resolution 13–14, 55, 59; avoidance of loss 98; facilitative 9, 73–5, 100–4, 109, 111–13, 130–1; unfair dismissal case vignette 116
resonance 54, 57
response-ability 36
responsibility 1, 9, 15–16, 22, 80; anxiety as the cost of 126; Bad Faith 36; blame and 98; for choosing 49, 52, 106; ethical issues 105; facilitative resolution 75, 131; family conflict case vignette 64, 66, 72; Heidegger 17; mediators 101, 107–8; principle of personal 73; temporality 43; unfair dismissal case vignette 125
retreat 12
rules of conduct 102

safety 109
Sartre, Jean-Paul 6, 17–18, 37, 80; Bad Faith and Good Faith 36, 41; choice 31; existence and essence 33; 'the look' 35, 38; the self 34
Schleiermacher, Friedrich 51, 53
self 27–8, 33–4, 48, 58
self-awareness 8, 14
self-concept 34–5, 78–9; emotions 83; family conflict case vignette 64; loss 111; safety 109; unfair dismissal case vignette 117, 124, 125; world-view 28, 30, 31
self-esteem 12, 28
silence 93
skills 89–94
Spinelli, E. 15, 31, 32, 45, 77, 80–1, 89, 108
'staying-with' 91, 92, 93, 112
Strasser, F. 27, 42, 74, 75

136 Index

strategies 95–9, 111
subjective truth 7, 73, 112, 129
submission 12

time/temporality 1, 15–16, 19–20,
39–43, 58–9; family conflict case
vignette 71; Heidegger 17;
mediation 112; re-choosing 32;
strategies 96–7
transience 31, 32, 40
trust 80, 95, 96, 109, 112, 125
truth 16, 17, 46, 49, 58, 127; contingency 54; developing 113;
hermeneutics 51; 'objective'
110; partiality and mutability 97;
respecting the truth of the other 99;
subjective 7, 73, 112, 129
'tuning in' and 'tuning out' 92, 96,
97, 112

Uberwelt 27, 28
Umwelt 27
uncertainty 1, 20, 22–3, 58, 79;
anxiety 29, 126; change and 31,
80; coping with 48; family conflict
case vignette 71; human contact 36;
intolerance of 49, 52; loss and 98;
phenomenology 45; time and 41
understanding 52, 54, 55
unfair dismissal case vignette 115–26
unfairness 12, 35, 71, 98, 99

values 7–8, 10, 22, 37, 75, 91;
acknowledgement of 109; adherence
to 32; avoidance of loss 98;
clarification of 102; competing
aspects 54, 128; compromise 81;
conflict resolution 73; contingency
48; emotions 30, 83, 85, 86, 129;
ethical issues 105, 106–7;

experience of 'facts' 101;
facilitative resolution 9; family conflict case vignette 70–1;
impediments to 111; maintenance
of 99; mediators 108; Nietzsche
16–17; realisation of 55; threats to
79; trust 95; world-views 13, 27–9,
49, 73, 77
Vedder, B. 53
violence 3
vulnerabilities 6, 80, 87, 95, 112;
exploration of 99; exposure of 54,
57; mediation process 103; power
issues 108; safety 109; unfair dismissal case vignette 120

Warnock, M. 36, 39
Weixel-Dixon, K. 42, 81
'win-win' situations 14, 112, 129
working alliance 74
workplace mediation 115–26
world, assumptions and values about
the 28, 48, 111
'worlding' 31
world-views 2, 12–14, 27–32, 57, 73,
77; actualisation of 17–18, 85–6;
avoidance of conflict 79–80;
challenges to 55; clarification of
10; competing aspects 54;
disruption of 127; emotions 84, 86,
87, 111; exploration of 95, 112,
113; family conflict case vignette
70, 71; maintenance of 99;
mediation 75; recognition of 9,
128; re-interpretation 46; safety
109; shifts in 48; trust 96; 'tuning
in' 92; unfair dismissal case
vignette 125–6; *see also*
aspirations; assumptions;
expectations; values